EuroMarketing

A Strategic Planner for SELLING into the NEW EUROPE

RICK ARONS

PROBUS PUBLISHING COMPANY
Chicago, Illinois

SLM

Library of Congress Cataloging-in-Publication Data

Arons, Rick.
  Euromarketing : a strategic planner for selling into the new Europe / Rick Arons.
    p. cm.
  Includes bibliographical references and index.
  ISBN 1-55738-201-8 : $27.50
    1. Export marketing — United States — Management. 2. United States — Commerce — Europe. 3. Europe — Commerce — United States. 4. Corporations, American — Europe. I. Title. II. Title : Euromarketing.
HF1416.5.A76 1992
658.8'48 — dc20   91-30334
                                                                CIP

Printed in the United States of America

ISBN 1-55738-201-8

BB

   2   3   4   5   6   7   8   9   0

For Marsha,

"She opens her mouth with wisdom, and a lesson of kindness is on her tongue."

Proverbs, Chapter 31, Verse 26

Table of Contents

List of Charts and Figures

Acknowledgements

While I have mentioned some by name in the text of this book, those who have contributed information, time and concern during the course of its writing deserve credit here.

Dr. Peter Rogge, Senior Vice President at the Swiss Bank Corporation in Basle, Switzerland, has provided both information and a framework in which to consider global change and the New Europe.

The international management consulting firm, Prognos AG (Basle), has cooperated by providing personal impressions of the changing face of European business. I would like to particularly thank Roland Bischoff for his concern, advice, and cooperation.

Colleagues in the United States have provided both discussion partners and valuable insight. In this regard, I would like to thank two Chicago-based businessmen, Ray Minkus, president of Weiser, Minkus, Walek Communications, Inc., as well as Paul Kohlenbrener of William M. Mercer, Inc..

Dr. Ernest Lebsanft, President of Synlogic AG of Basle, Switzerland, provided profiles of smaller American and European companies in the artificial intelligence field, while Dr. Norbert Schroder of Intechno Consulting shared his technical perspective.

Thanks also to Klaus Amann of Amann Industrial Software of Mainz, Germany, and Peter Wetzer and

Achim Zerressen of Endress & Hauser, Reinach, Switzerland. The people at Probus Publishing Company ought to know that their confidence has been appreciated. Many others, too numerous to name here, from companies around the United States were kind enough to respond to my questionnaires.

I also want to be careful to credit Mrs. Beatrice Arons as the source for an anecdote or two, as well as for her tireless support. Thanks and credit are due to H'K"B"H for allowing me to accomplish this project.

R.A., December, 1990

I
INTRODUCTION

1 *The Three Telephones*

S ome time ago, former British Prime Minister
Margaret Thatcher attended a celebration at the
White House.

As the evening wore on and the crowd began to
thin out, the remaining guests entered the Oval Office
to chat briefly about economic and social concerns.
Distracted by images of the rooms and offices she had
just visited, Mrs. Thatcher was unable to focus on the
conversation at hand. As her eyes wandered about the
room, the President turned in his chair, revealing three
telephones on the cabinet behind him. Each was a different color—the first one, red; the second, black; and
the third, white.

Her curiousity aroused, she held her thoughts until
the meeting had concluded and the other guests had left.
Then, alone with her host, she asked for a description of
the function of each phone. The President obliged, explaining that the red phone was a direct line to the
Kremlin, the black phone a direct line to the Pentagon,
and the white phone a direct line to Heaven.

Noting no hint of humor in the President's voice,
Mrs. Thatcher asked if she could use the white phone.
The President acquiesced, and left Mrs. Thatcher alone
in his office. On picking up the phone, the Prime Minister was overjoyed to find herself speaking directly to

3

the man in charge. Ten minutes later she replaced the receiver and emerged from the Oval Office. The President then returned, and presented her with a bill for the cost of the call, explaining that in these days of worrisome budget deficits, no cost of doing business could be overlooked. Mrs. Thatcher took a crisp new American ten dollar bill from her purse, exactly the charge for the heavenly call she had made, and handed it to the President.

Not much later, Mrs. Thatcher was called to Brussels for a meeting of the heads of state of the twelve member governments of the European Community. The gathering was presided over by Jacques Delors, President of the EC and a Frenchman. After some hours, the meeting was concluded. Monsieur Delors invited several of the attendees back to his office in order to continue discussing several issues of pressing concern. Mrs. Thatcher joined this group in order to make sure that the full weight of British "good sense" could be brought to bear in any discussion of European economic or social policy that might threaten the independence of her country.

As M. Delors shifted positions in his desk chair, Mrs. Thatcher was taken by a familiar sight. On the credenza behind M. Delors were three telephones, identical to those she had seen in the Oval Office in Washington, D.C. some time before. She waited patiently for the meeting to break up and for her colleagues to disband. Before leaving, she briefly chatted with M. Delors and inquired about the phones. M. Delors casually replied that the red phone was a direct line to the Kremlin, the black phone a direct line to NATO headquarters, and the white phone, a direct line to Heaven.

Her heart racing, Mrs. Thatcher asked whether she might use the white telephone. M. Delors acceded and excused himself while Mrs. Thatcher called and carried on a ten-minute conversation with The Man Upstairs. As she returned the receiver to its place and emerged from the office she was immediately confronted by M. Delors who presented her with a bill for the phone charges, explaining that the EC was being funded by all of the member governments, and therefore had to account carefully for all expenditures. As she reached for her purse, Mrs. Thatcher noticed that the charge for the call was less than one ECU (less than an American dollar)! Incredulous, she asked M. Delors how this call could cost so little, particularly in light of the cost of her earlier call from the White House in the United States. Unshaken by the comparison, M. Delors casually replied that for an American, a call to Heaven is long-distance indeed. But for a Frenchman, it is considered a local call!

No Single Strategy for the Single Market

Europe is not simply an agglomeration of small (by American standards) nations, but is a group of diverse and distinct national and ethnic groups. Each fiercely protects its independent national history and unique cultural heritage at any cost. In this light, the phenomenon which is the European Community is remarkable. That these intensely proud people, who battled each other for hundreds of years, would now band together for the general economic good is testimony to the economic desperation that each nation must feel.

The French remain a singular curiosity. There is little chance of the European Community overwhelming the French language or culture. The French have taken every opportunity to lean against the wind, even to the extent that a such a position may threaten the unity of the larger group. The French military marches to its own drummer. It has withheld support from NATO, while conducting its own defense policy and diplomacy. As the military threat from Eastern Europe subsided, Jean-Pierre Chevenement, fromer French Minister of Defense, announced on Bastille Day, 1990, his intent to build a strong French military independent of NATO. While the announcement was cloaked in warnings about the instability of Eastern Europe, the fact that France is the world's third largest weapons exporter was not lost on its allies. Nothing so mundane as the end of the "Cold War" will be allowed to destroy the French defense industry.

Such independence is not limited to the French. A surge of German nationalism followed the collapse of the Berlin Wall. Young and old, those Germans with memories of a pre-World War II nation and those without, sought immediate reunification. Germans, who already had a strong influence over the fiscal and technical policies of the Community, saw their political stars rising to unprecedented heights. Nationalistic euphoria overwhelmed the cost of unification.

The clearly-drawn cultural lines established in Europe have encouraged stereotypes. Research done in seven European countries by the Chamber of Commerce of Rouen found that if companies were not able to fill a middle or senior level management job at home, only 25% would advertise elsewhere in the EC—and even then, would consider only certain countries.

For example,[1] a survey of 700 British companies found the following national recruitment preferences:

- 35% thought that German and Dutch managers would be the most compatible with their own,

- 33% liked the French,

- 25% liked the Belgians, and

- 14% preferred the Italians and Spanish.

One German headhunter was quoted as saying that "Italians and Mediterraneans don't meet German standards of high work and quality." He also said, "The Swiss are too expensive, too demanding and want to be in charge immediately."

So what does all of this mean in terms of the "New Europe?" It means that once having overcome the intangible barriers to entry to the Single Market, there will be a constant need for corporate vigilance. The forces that would divide Europe are nearly as strong as those that strive to hold it together. An economic crisis that precipitates a war of words among the member states could well degenerate into the suspension and change of directives and regulations in individual markets.

While movement toward a Single European Market is a signal to look at trade opportunities in a new light, success will be dictated by cultural and political adaptation, a thoughtful analysis of competitors and competitive strategies, and a realistic assessment of one's assets and liabilities. This new and changing market will push successful players toward partnerships and market niches which will lead to long-term success and integration as full and equal participants in otherwise protected markets.

2 *Resurrecting a Kingdom in Decline*

Imagine yourself king of all that you survey. You are a benevolent ruler, allowing certain freedoms that do not infringe upon the conduct of state business or upon the centralized control that you have imposed.

Your domain has a rich, long history. Generations upon generations have worked the fields, developed the land, produced food and shelter and, clothing, energy, and the other staples of society.

You maintain a standing army, which has protected your borders, and has suppressed those who would seek a new form of government. You have developed alliances with your neighboring principalities, each of whom has a vested interest in the maintenance of its independence, and each of whom has a proud history like your own. Empires have risen and fallen, but still, your kingdom survives, outlasting even the most dominating among them.

As the decades have passed, your native industries have continued to produce, but their progress has been retarded (Figure 1).

FIGURE 1:   THE EUROPEAN KINGDOM IN DECLINE (1982-1986)

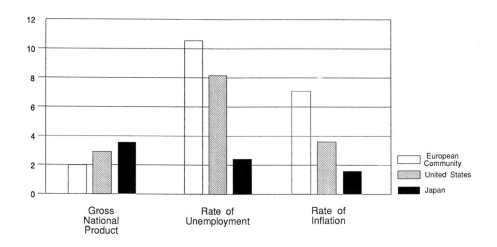

Source: European Community

Your gross domestic product has increased at a rate far less than that of your principal international competitors. Your share of the world market in such industries as electrical goods, motor vehicles, machinery, and data processing equipment has fallen against those of the more productive countries in the West and Far East (Figure 2). Your level of productivity and that of your neighboring states is only a fraction of that of the much feared Far Eastern Empire (Figure 3). The incentive to become efficient and more globally competitive with those who produce comparable foreign goods has been stifled by both tax laws and import and export levies originally intended to protect home-grown, bedrock industries. Job maintenance has been won at the cost of global competitiveness. Your taxes and levies have created a large and influential class of civil servants who control the direction and pace of industrial and social policy.

FIGURE 2:   DECLINING EUROPEAN MARKET SHARE
Losses (-) of market share by the European community in third
countries over the period 1979-85 (in descending order)

Industry	Loss
Electrical goods	-4.39
Motor vehicles	-4.25
Rubber and plastic products	-2.53
Industrial and agricultural machinery	-2.49
Other transport equipment	-2.27
Office and data-processing machines, precision and optical instruments	-2.23
Other manufactured products	-0.84
Metal products, except machinery and transport equipment	-0.65

Source: European Commission Services

Your throne has been the rallying point for an unusually high level of patriotism. Nationalistic sentiment pervades every area of the economic and social landscape. Industrial purchases are made at home from producers who manufacture their products at home. A social contract has been put in place that values the possession of a livelihood above the nature of that livelihood. The face that your countrymen present to their neighboring principalities is one of unity and pride in your national heritage, language, and culture. Your national institutions have been preserved at all costs, jobs saved, and industry perpetuated.

But, your role has changed over time. You once had a hand in the direction of every significant social, military, or economic activity of you kingdom. With the wars and revolutions around you, you recognized the need to yield power to loyal subjects — to grant them a level of autonomy heretofore unheard of in the land. For only four or five decades, your subjects have been selecting representatives from among their peers to represent them in a legislative body. While it does not

FIGURE 3:   THE LAG IN EUROPEAN PRODUCTIVITY
Level of productivity in the United Kingdom, France, FRG
and Japan-1985 (USA=100)

	UK	France	Germany (West)	Japan
Strong demand sectors				
Electrical and electronic goods	28	47	43	236
Office and data-processing machines	37	43	45	94
Chemical and pharmaceutical products	54	79	75	119
Moderate demand sectors				
Transport equipment	23	54	60	95
Food, beverages, tobacco	56	73	47	37
Paper and printing prodcuts	43	67	76	89
Industrial and agricultural machinery	20	49	46	103
Weak demand sectors				
Metal products	38	60	54	143
Ferrous and non-ferrous ores and metals	66	72	92	149
Textiles, leather, clothing	59	62	71	53
Non-metallic mineral (construction materials)	40	64	71	43
Total prodcutivity	42	65	65	100

Source: European Commisssion Services

tamper with the constitution itself, it does create and modify the rules that direct the daily activities of the land.

The role of your kingdom in the greater scheme of things has also changed. Alliances have developed, both political and economic, and it has been to your advantage to join them in order to protect your realm from military aggression. More recently, you can't have failed to notice your flagging economic fortunes.

New economic powers have arisen and they threaten the viability of your own industry. Products and services whose quality and formulation far exceed those of your own have invaded your markets and already steal a large share of business formerly held by local enterprises. Your legislators have acted to staunch the bleeding by enacting laws that block the influx of outside products and services. Quotas have been put in place and border levies have been enacted. Given this protection, local industry breathes a collective sigh of relief.

A Common Market to the Rescue

But the cure may be worse than the disease. Your industry continues to fall further behind those Eastern and Western international competitors. Industrialists from both of these competing societies have become heavy investors both in your kingdom and in the economies of the surrounding states. Entire industries are becoming dominated by foreign products or investment. Both your citizens and those of the neighboring states realize that better and cheaper products and services are available, but that within the borders of your kingdom protective regulation is keeping them out of reach.

While your countrymen do their best to fight off the foreign competition, the problem is exacerbated by the fact that each of your neighbors confronts the same set of economic difficulties. Your government has been holding a series of meetings with neighboring states in order to formulate a joint response.

For years, your kingdom had been the leading manufacturer of widgets in the world. No widgetech can be constructed without one of your widgets. With every household in the developed world having at least one widgetech, your kingdom has led a charmed existence, generating plenty of foreign exchange, and enjoying a high standard of living. Widgets have been produced at home and exported, providing a steady source of employment in your kingdom. As much as 80 percent of the world widget market is controlled by the crown jewel of your kingdom's industrial base, Widget Systems Unlimited. In turn, a majority of the ownership of WSU is held by your government.

This was all very comforting until about ten years ago when a less developed, third-world country got hold of a new widget design and a streamlined, automated production process for its manufacture. Since that time, that country and its low-cost labor force have severely cut into your market share. From a world market share in excess of 80 percent, WSU now controls only 25 percent of the world market for widgets. And that share is still falling. Your own history has conspired against you. Your artificially high labor content in production has begun to price your product out of the market. At the same time, the quality advantage that WSU once enjoyed has been eliminated by technological advances made by more productive workers with greater performance and social incentives. The repercussions of this tidal change in the economy have been felt in every sector.

WSU, employer of nearly one-quarter of your subjects, has seen its overhead rise with time while its revenue base shrinks. While it monopolizes its home market, its share of neighboring markets has fallen dramatically.

Recognizing that your neighboring principalities have been feeling the same combination of external and internal pressures, you urge your government to pursue a series of summit meetings with neighboring states to discuss common problems and arrive at potential solutions. As a result, an economic union is created to foster change, enhance competition, and prepare the way for a general balancing of neighboring economies where earnings, taxes and noneconomic barriers needn't stand in the way of common trade and economic incentive.

Things seem to be progressing nicely, but those same external raiders, the Mongols in the East and the

barbarians from the West, continue to insinuate themselves into your economy to an alarming degree. The
New Economic Union is losing control of its own des-
tiny. The competitive stance is improving, and incentives for technical and market improvements are in
place. Nevertheless, your region needs to buy time for
its industries to recover and become globally competitive again.

Your government clearly understands the choices.
Salvation seems to be associated with increasingly
closer ties to your neighbors. Your people have little
choice but to risk a loss of national sovereignty and,
ultimately, a dilution of a treasured, centuries-old culture.

Of course, the New Economic Union still must be
tested during the hard times. What will happen to its
cooperative programs when its results are uneven. How
will your government and citizens respond to the prosperity of neighboring industry at their expense? How
many layoffs will your now privatized widget industry
tolerate before shutting the door to exports? How much
control of your own economy are you going to give up
before you put your foot down and say, "no more?" Are
you willing to accept a currency without your picture on
it? Will your legislators continue to cede power to a
bunch of bureaucrats located in a distant city, in a
neighboring country?

For the short-term there is little doubt that your
kingdom is better off as a result of the collective effort
being made. Your New Economic Union is pursuing its
own idea of economic and political efficiency. The rest
of the world will just have to understand that the rules
have changed and, in doing so, adapt to a new economic,
political, and social order.

3

How Much Do You Know About the "New Europe"?

Recent international testing of both school-age children and their parents indicates that Americans are hard-pressed to distinguish between Madrid and Munich, much less the cultural differences between their citizens.

We now live in what has quickly become a "one-world" economy, demanding an awareness of and sensitivity to the geography and culture of the world around us, and, ideally, a keen interest in and understanding of what is important to our alter egos across the globe.

Imagine for a moment that a close friend of yours—a former roommate at Parsons College—has spent the past several years running a sleepy but successful family textile business in Gloversville, New York. Having just completed an MBA in four years of evening sessions at Albany State University, he is looking for new markets for his line of winter gloves and high-fashion socks. He has phoned you after reading an article in *Fortune Magazine* touting the opportunities ahead for apparel manufacturers in the growing Spanish and European markets.

Your friend admits to knowing little about Europe or the European Community, and has contacted you, a vice president at a money-center bank in the Midwest, for some advice. You've spent the better part of your career advising clients on domestic financing and yet, you now find an increasing thirst among your middle market customers for "perspective" about the "New Europe."

What do you really know about this "New Europe"? In order to respond to your former roommate, you should already have a base of knowledge absorbed through the daily and periodic business press. How much work are you going to need to do to become sufficiently knowledgeable about Single Market Europe to be of help to both your friend and your middle market clients? In order to determine just where on the learning curve you sit, a short quiz has been provided. A score of twenty-five or more correct answers is admirable and is indicative of your already considerable conversational knowledge of the subject. Fewer than twenty correct answers sheds a great deal of doubt upon your attention to the daily media. You are going to need some tutoring. Answer fewer than ten of the following questions correctly, and the results of this quiz are automatically forwarded to your employer.

A Quiz to Test Your Knowledge

Let's talk about us

1. What country has the greatest share of total world exports?
    a. U.S.A.   b. Japan   c. West Germany   d. Finland

2. Shoppers from which of the regions below were the greatest per capita consumers of American-made products in 1989?
    a. Japan   b. West Germany, Italy, & France   c. Canada   d. Sri Lanka

3. Average labor costs are the lowest in which of the following countries?
   a. United Kingdom   b. U.S.A.   c. West Germany   d. Italy

4. Over the past twenty years, U.S. companies have sold in aggregate this much heavy electrical equipment to the utility companies of the twelve European Community member countries:
   a. 0   b. $100 million   c. $1 billion   d. $10 billion

5. The service sector employs about 75 percent of the U.S. labor force. What is the comparable percentage in the European Community?
   a. 25 percent   b. 40 percent   c. 60 percent   d. 80 percent

Looking at the Single Market

6. According to a 1989 A.T. Kearney survey, what was the primary goal of a typical company building a new facility in Europe?
   a. Cost reduction   b. Quality improvement   c. Enhanced delivery & service   d. Market share growth

7. Plant shutdowns lasting as long as one month are not uncommon in Europe.
   True   False

8. Which of these is not an official language of the European Community?
   a. Dutch   b. Danish   c. Portuguese   d. Greek   e. Swedish

9. This country has the lowest rate of inflation in the European Community.
   a. Ireland   b. Luxembourg   c. West Germany   d. The Netherlands

10. Because of its rapid growth, relatively inexpensive labor, and nice weather, this country is referred to as the "California of Europe."
    a. Greece   b. Portugal   c. Spain   d. Italy

11. This European country has the Continent's longest history of business franchising.
    a. France   b. West Germany   c. United Kingdom   d. Italy

The Terminology of Trade

12. Rules of Origin contain reference to:
    a. the birth place of an EC citizen.
    b. the last substantial source of a product's makeup and identity.
    c. the resolution of patent rights among competing national claims.
    d. the headquarters location of an operating company.

13. EFTA is the:
     a. Economic Facility and Transport Association.
     b. European Federation of Tariff Associations.
     c. European Free Trade Association.

14. CEN/CENELEC is:
     a. a union of European political organizations from the twelve EC member
        states.
     b. the most popular golf/country club complex in France.
     c. a pair of European technical standard setting organizations.

15. A European Currency Unit (ECU) is equal to approximately how many
     drachmas (December 1990)?
     a. 10   b. 25   c. 84   d. 192   e. It's Greek to me!

16. What is Cabotage?
     a. The transport of both passengers and goods on the same vehicle
     b. The transport of cargo between points within a country
     c. The transport of goods between points in different countries
     d. A leafy green vegetable exported by the Danish

The European Community Represents a $4 Trillion Economy

17. More of the fifty most profitable companies in Europe come from this country
     than any other.
     a. France   b. West Germany   c. Great Britian   d. Italy

18. This industry represents 3 percent of the European Community's GDP. Nearly
     60 percent of all jobs in the EC are either directly or indirectly linked to it.
     a. Energy   b. Transportation   c. Telecommunications   d. Tourism

19. The percentage of components of American origin found in European auto-
     mobiles is:
     a. increasing.   b. decreasing.   c. remaining about the same.

20. Five major automobile companies produce more than one million cars per year
     in this EC member country.
     a. France   b. West Germany   c. Belgium   d. Italy

21. In the mid-1980s, the average cost of telecommunications equipment and services in Europe was this much greater than its cost in the U.S.
a. 10 percent   b. 50 percent   c. 100 percent   d. 1,000 percent

22. The cellular telephone market in Europe now relies primarily on this technology.
a. Digital   b. Analog   c. Animal   d. Vegetable

23. After December 31, 1992, American exporters to the EC will be under great pressure to ship on open account (without insisting on letters of credit).
True   False

24. The average annual number of hours worked by a West German laborer in 1989 was 1697. This is the lowest figure among EC member states. Which member state had the highest average?
a. Italy   b. Spain   c. Belgium   d. United Kingdom

25. This EC member state has provided its industry with more anti- competitive subsidies than any other.
a. Italy   b. Denmark   c. France   d. Portugal

Know Your Competition!

26. The largest European supplier of electrical connectors, with three production plants in West Germany, and six elsewhere in Europe is:
a. AMP (U.S.)   b. Thomson (France)   c. Philips (Netherlands)
d. General Electric Co. (U.K.)

27. This company is Europe's largest electronics company with over 300 operating businesses and a product line of over 200,000 items.
a. Siemens   b. Philips   c. Thomson   d. Matra

28. "Cross-Country Marketing" is a strategy:
a. for the promotion and sale of short skis throughout the EC.
b. for the development of a common marketing approach for all EC units.
c. to allow a single sales team to market to units of a single parent company when the units are in different geographic markets.

Bonus Questions

29. Berlaymount is:
    a. the president of the European Commission.
    b. the name of the oddly shaped EC headquarters building in Brussels.
    c. the NATO code name for the European Community.
    d. the highest peak on the Iberian Peninsula.

30. What is the Val Duchesse Dialogue?
    a. The compiled text of the proceedings of the European Parliament.
    b. A series of meetings on social issues between management and labor aimed at influencing EC social policy.
    c. The dialogue from the final act of the "Phantom of the Opera."

Has your friend contacted the right person? Can you give him the help he is looking for? If not, continue reading. Let's see just how quickly you can bring yourself up to speed.

Answers to the Quiz: How Much Do You Know About the New Europe?

1. a	2. a	3. a	4. a	5. c	6. a	7. True	8. e
9. d	10. c	11. a	12. b	13. c	14. c	15. d	16. b
17. c	18. c	19. a	20. c	21. c	22. b	23. True	24. b
25. a	26. a	27. a	28. c	29. b	30. b		

4

Danger: Continent Under Construction— Proceed at Your Own Risk

In the wake of both industrial and demographic cycles that have laid waste to large tracts of industrial America, localities and states have struggled to attract business investment that can bring both employment growth and economic vitality.

The lesson of the American economic development experience is clear. Anyone who is prepared to invest in a particular region of the United States and, who in doing so will create jobs, is not simply welcome, but is hunted down like a dog. Those Japanese and European companies who seek manufacturing locations in the U.S., often find themselves caught among warring states and localities—each showering the prospective newcomer with promises of tax relief, investment and job credits and outright grants.

A great deal of discussion is devoted to the notion that foreign firms are buying up American real estate, businesses, and strategic resources at an alarming rate. As a practical matter, however, little real interest exists in biting the hand that is feeding so many of us.

When an American businessman sees the typically American investment incentives being offered in Europe by local and state governments, the potential investor quite naturally expects to be received in much the same way that his foreign counterpart is received in the U.S. At first blush, the experience seems quite comparable. There is even a body of supporting statistical evidence documenting the excesses. Some economic development experts have estimated, for example, that the British spent the equivalent of $85,000 in subsidies for every new job created in the early 1980s. [1]

The British spent the equivalent of $85,000 in subsidies for every new job created in the early 1980s

Are appearances deceiving? Is the process of investment in Europe in the context of the completion of the Single Market comparable to the American economic development experience over the last decade? Europeans have taken an ambivalent view of foreign investment at home—encouraging it in some cases and discouraging it in others (Figure 4).

As one would expect, large European national champions jealously protect their own investment incentives while complaining about the encouragement of increased American and Japanese investment. In the 1990 fiscal year, the Japanese invested $14.4 billion in the EC—a 74 percent increase from 1989 and seven times the level of 1985. [2] One-half of that total was used to purchase European companies. The French have been outspoken in their expression of a certain resentment of the Japanese presence. During a state visit to France in 1990, Japanese Prime Minister Toshiki Kaifu listened while then Euro-

Industry leaders are demanding new EC rules that would disallow investment grants to Japanese and Americans

FIGURE 4:   PROJECTED INVESTMENT GROWTH IN THE EC

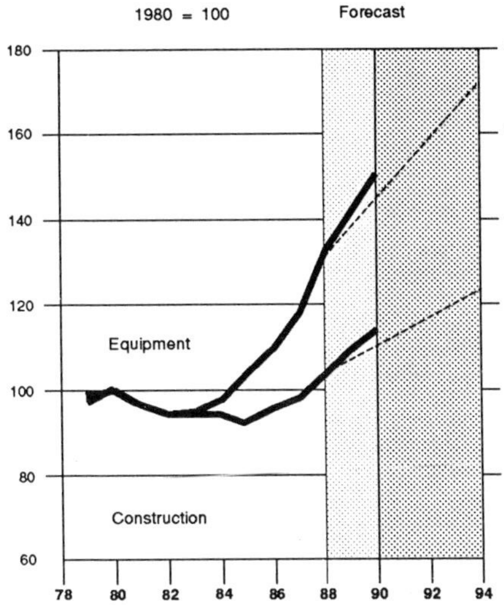

1) W. Germany, France, Italy, UK, Spain, Belgium, Netherlands
At 1980 prices and exchange rates

Source: EURO-INVEST, 89

pean Affairs Minister, Edith Cresson, described Japan as having "an absolute desire to conquer the world" (Figure 5).

SGS-Thomson Microelectronics chairman, Pasquale Pistorio, has called foreign investment in his industry "colonization." He and other industry leaders are demanding new EC rules that would disallow investment grants to Japanese and Americans, encouraging regions and localities to compete for their foreign investment. He points to a Texas Instruments Italia SpA, four year, $1.2 billion investment program with the Italian government aimed at increasing its MOS memory chip capacity at its existing plant.

SGS-Thomson has a French-Italian venture that is getting very little support from the Italian government, and the company feels that the Italian government is irresponsibly helping the foreign competition. Pistorio claims that the large Italian TI investment is, in reality, creating very few jobs. At the same time, by strengthen-

FIGURE 5:   DIRECT INVESTMENT BY THE JAPANESE IN EUROPE

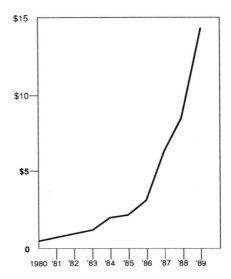

Source: Japanese Ministry of Finance

ing the American competition, the Italian government is risking the jobs of thousands of Italians working in Pistorio's company[3] (Figure 6 and 7).

If the degree of American investment necessary to establish and maintain market share in Europe raises a Continental backlash, will the door to the EC market place be closed completely? When the growth spurt associated with the completion of the Single Market is interrupted by continuing economic downturns, will there still be an opportunity for American firms to operate in an unrestricted market place?

> *If American investment raises a Continental backlash, will the door to the EC market be closed completely?*

Intel is being "forced" to invest over $400 million in a semiconductor plant near Dublin, at least partly as a result of a 1989 EC directive concerning the application of local content and domestic origin rules for semiconductors. Local manufacturing of its IC's will relieve

FIGURE 6:   U.S. DIRECT INVESTMENT 1988

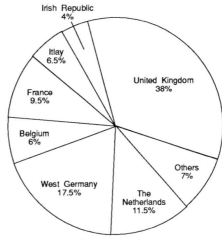

Total Investment: U.S. $127.8 billion

Source: U.S. Department of Commerce

FIGURE 7:   FOREIGN-OWNED MANUFACTURING PLANTS IN THE EC (1988)

	U.S.-owned	Japanese-owned
United Kingdom	669	92
West Germany	363	67
France	291	85
Italy	208	24
Netherlands	186	27
Belguim	182	23
Ireland	147	19
Spain	136	41
Denmark	32	2
Portugal	26	7
Greece	19	4
Luxembourg	17	23

Source: U.S. Department of Commerce

Intel of a fourteen percent EC tariff (the U.S., Japan, and Canada do not tariff these items). The strategy ramifications for Intel are significant. The company has decided to stop licensing other companies to make its microprocessors, and many of the former licensees are retaliating by acquiring rights to produce competitive chips. Seven of the world's largest semiconductor manufacturers (European, Japanese, and American) have joined forces in an effort to rest market leadership from Intel.

The introduction of captive manufacturing in Europe places Intel in an entirely new competitive landscape—a landscape littered with political requirements. It is unlikely that rules of origin will play any less a political role in European-American business in the future either. Complain though we may, American firms should be careful about pointing fingers. As many as nineteen different rules of origin are on the American trade books.[4] These include the General Substantial Transformation Rule, Insular Possessions Treatment, anti-dumping measures, the Buy-America program, voluntary restraint programs for automobiles and steel, and many more. Ultimately, relief on either side of the Atlantic is going to be reciprocal or non-existent.

Can we be certain that, in just a few years, an American firm will be given the option of locating a manufacturing plant within the EC if the proposed plant will compete directly with local industry? While the idea may now seem far-fetched, the economic landscape could change quite quickly. In 1989, European companies were busy cutting costs and consolidating. Groupe Bull announced the elimination of 1,200 jobs, Nixdorf Computer, 5,000, and British Telecom, 1,400. N.V. Philips with 340,000 employees worldwide, began cutting costs by $375 million in 1988. Included were 20,000 middle management jobs, the closings of seventy European plants and the

After completion of the Single Market, will Brussels be so tolerant of business failure or employment loss at the hands of non-EC competitors?

transfer of some production to the Far East. Such cuts may be competitive in nature, and the economy may have the resiliency to pick up some of the employment slack. However, after the completion of the Single Market, will Brussels be so tolerant of business failure or employment loss at the hands of non-EC-based competitors?

Even the acquisition of a European company can be left in question. While the EC has a directive in place allowing its review of large mergers and acquisitions, the Treaty of Rome specifically limits EC authority in "competition policy." As a consequence, member states have the right to take measures "to protect legitimate interests" other than competition. This may well be used as the rationale to review all of a country's mergers for reason of State interest. The competition directive itself states that when a country can make the case that the proposed merger affects the uniqueness or "distinct marketing patterns" in that country, the national government has the right to interdict a proposed business combination.

There are already a variety of barriers in place on the national level that may preclude American acquisitions of European firms. For example, in Germany, a brief list of impediments to foreign acquisition includes statutory employee rights, limits on the transfer of shares and voting rights, the near impossibility of removing a company board, and the often large shareholdings of German banks in an acquisition candidate. Germany has institutionalized the family business as well. While there are thousands of publicly held companies in the United States, there are fewer than 500 in Germany (1990). Inheritance laws and taxes are such that a company owner must leave the bulk of his wealth to his immediate family. The maximum inheritance tax for the wife and children is about 35 percent while for others, 70 percent.

Germany has institutionalized the family business.

It should come as no surprise that 75 percent of the EC companies acquired by outsiders are British.

The tenor of national anti-trust legislation is quite different from EC member state to EC member state. The German Federal Cartel Office uses a pure competition criterion based on market share and industry concentration to measure merger proposals. The British and Irish combine the competition criterion with a group of national industrial objectives. France has its own national industrial policy and wants to promote large, integrated national companies. In doing so, little attention is paid to market concentrations. So, in the face of an EC policy that intends to promote pan- European mergers, local policies can be sufficiently restrictive so that almost any logical business combination can, for national reasons, be overridden.

It should come as no surprise that 75 percent of the EC companies acquired by outsiders are British.

Both the U.S. and Europe have the "anti-dumping" weapon at their protectionist disposal. In the ball bearing field, for example, the U.S. has been threatened by European imports for several years. Timken and Torrington finally managed to get the U.S. International Trade Commission to impose duties of over 200% on certain kinds of ball bearings from Sweden, West Germany and Italy. Nevertheless, the dumpers have managed to circumvent such penalties in their entirety by shipping merchandise to third countries who then re-ship to the U.S.

The proper American response to lost market share is to force up the cost of doing business at the source.

The proper American response to lost market share is to force up the cost of doing business at the source—in Europe—by competing more effectively there. In doing so, however, it is quite likely that the very same sorts of penalties may be elicited as protection for Europe's domestic industry.

Interestingly, while foreign cars occupy a worrisomely large part of the American automobile market, the percentage of U.S. components in European cars is quietly increasing. It is just a matter of time until the EC looks more closely at the source of its high technology automotive components. Electronic and diagnostic systems are increasingly imported or purchased from the European subsidiaries of U.S. companies. If European industry fails to meet the need, will a protectionist, institutional reaction be inevitable? France convinced the European Commission to temporarily block imports of Japanese and South Korean TV sets via other member states who have more liberal import policies. Italy had the EC impose a similar measure against Japanese sewing machines. Slowing European economic growth and the accompanying shortfall in EC revenues, taken against a backdrop of static or increasing EC commitments to Eastern Europe, could make the case for more protection incontrovertible.

By American standards, the economic history of Europe is one of "selective protectionism" for inefficient and politically sensitive commercial interests. The EC has preserved this system by implementing a series of transition rules which extend protection over certain product classes in specific member countries. These QR's (quantitative restrictions) in Europe can mean more competition in the U.S. for manufacturers who must divert production away from Europe. On the other hand, in a quest for uniformity, the EC may, for example, force France and Italy to relax their VRA's (Voluntary Restraint Agreements) on Korean or Taiwanese shoes. Should this occur, it could quite negatively affect exports of American shoes to the EC. In 1989, 65 percent of U.S. footwear exports to the EC went to France and Italy.[5] The increased competition from lower-cost Asian producers could be a blow to U.S. manufacturers.

Meanwhile, we Americans may be a bit overconfident about our own business acumen and its ability to carry the day in Europe. According to a *Fortune Maga-*

The economic history of Europe is one of "Selective Protectionism."

zine survey of corporate executives[6] 67 percent of those responding believe that U.S. companies are more competitive with European and Japanese companies than they were five years ago.

Americans may be overconfident about their ability to carry the day in Europe.

A 1989 A.T. Kearney survey found that the primary goal for American companies planning new facilities was to lower their costs—and this at a time when customers continue to increase their emphasis on quality and service. This customer emphasis is even more pronounced in Europe. In a study produced by Pittiglio, Rabin, Todd & McGrath for the American Electronics Association in early 1990, American electronics companies were sternly criticized for their inability to address the critical competitive factors of quality management and time-to-market (TTM). Fewer than one-quarter of the 250 companies surveyed had implemented corporate quality programs. For those with a Total Quality Management (TQM) program in place, an average improvement of 25 percent in product quality (based on defects) was achieved over the previous three years. According to Pittiglio, Rabin, Todd & McGrath, this is less than one-half of the improvement that a good TQM program should achieve over that period. In terms of TTM—a competitive factor that 93 percent of the surveyed companies rated as critical—only 5 percent of the companies had made improvements at all. The study implies a continued decline in the global competitiveness of American electronics firms.

The study implies a continued decline in the global competitiveness of American electronics firms.

And yet, in a 1989 survey of subscribers to *Electronic Business*,[7] 95 percent of its respondents claimed to be doing business in Europe already—38 percent already manufactured in Europe while 45 percent expected to be making some products in Europe by the end of that year. A KPMG Peat Marwick survey showed that 50 percent of the executives surveyed expected to increase R&D in Europe in the near term. Bold planning, but is it too little, too late?

A survey of European engineering managers taken by EDN magazine showed that 35 percent expected to make fewer purchases from U.S. companies and that 83 percent planned to make more purchases from European suppliers. The results of a poll of members of the British Parliament taken in late 1988 showed that 65 percent of the MP's felt that barriers to exports by outsiders would increase after 1992—56 percent saying that it would be harder to export to the U.K. and 66 percent stating that U.S. firms should worry about being discriminated against in industry purchasing decisions in general.[8]

Eighty-three percent of European engineering managers plan to make more purchases from European suppliers.

The economics of competing with the Europeans can be daunting as well. While to some extent, the differences in labor cost, particularly in several of the EC member markets, is narrowing, the cost of capital is considerably greater for American companies than for their European counterparts. The Japanese also have a distinct advantage in this area in their quest for European expansion. Federal Reserve Bank of New York figures show that from 1983 to 1988, the cost of capital for U.S. companies was twice that of their West German and Japanese competitors. In the same period, Japanese bank loans rose 200 percent while U.S. bank loans rose only 11 percent. The Japanese market share of international commercial financing doubled to 40 percent while the U.S. market share fell from 27 percent to 15 percent. Certain operating conditions are changing as well—and forever. The tried and true procedure of exporting to the EC and expecting a letter of credit in return may soon disappear. It is likely that after 1992, exporters will have to ship on open account. Credit insurance, export factoring, and good credit research will be indispensable.

The cost of capital for U.S. companies was twice that of their German and Japanese competitors.

It may seem hard to believe (particularly if you are involved in agriculture), but Europe is even more reliant on business subsidies than we are here in America. The research programs described elsewhere in this book represent only a small portion of the subsidization of private industry by both the EC and its member state governments. GATT agreements not withstanding, such direct and indirect subsidies will continue to give European firms an unusual advantage over outsiders. The EC discovered in 1989, for example, that 3 percent of its annual GDP was being distributed in the form of government subsidies. Some countries were even discovered to have given out more than they took back in taxes. While subsidies are being reduced, they remain a substantial impediment to the equal participation of outside firms in the Internal Market (Figure 8).

> *In 1989, the EC disbursed $100 billion in government subsidies.*

FIGURE 8:   EC MEMBER STATE PUBLIC SUBSIDIES

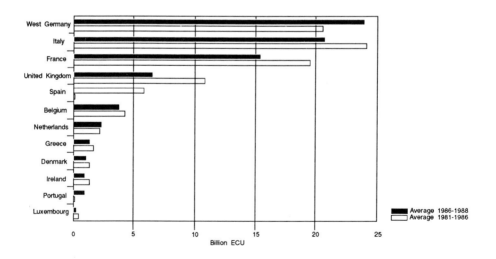

Source: European Commission
"Second Survey on State Aids," July 31, 1990

The Italian government was found to be the biggest abuser of anti-competitive subsidies. The West German government gave away $45 billion in domestic subsidies (3.6 percent of the GDP) in 1989—three times the level of the U.S.

In trying to control these national subsidies, the EC at one point, blocked a $7 million subsidy for a SmithKline Biological SA, $130 million Belgian plant investment. At the same time, the EC approved a $110 million French government subsidy of a Chantiers Navals de St. Nazaire defense bid, and a $850 million subsidy from the British government to its shipyards.

In trying to control national subsidies, the EC blocked a Belgian grant to SmithKline Biological.

British Satellite Broadcasting claims that Societe Europeenne des Satellites is getting special incentives (including ten years of tax exemptions and state-guaranteed bank loans of eighty million ECU's). France and the Netherlands got in trouble for subsidizing Renault and Volvo respectively. The EC felt that the arrangements and loans gave the companies an unfair advantage over the competition. Spain has thirty-two separate subsidy plans to allot funds specifically to the automotive industry. Firms in the Netherlands can apply for subsidies equal to 16.22 percent of each Research and Development worker's gross salary.

Bending to the hysteria of the German Green Party in 1989, the European Community placed a moratorium on the anabolic steroid, BST (bovine somatropin), and as a result, on all beef raised with such growth hormones. The ban affected dairy products produced with BST as well. But, the BST controversy is more than just an environmental concern. The economic ramifications of the import of beef from large, healthy American cows touch on the very survival of the small European farmer. Lower milk prices based on the increased supply of these more efficient cows could put a number of such dairy farmers out of business. Environmental (read: economic) concerns are real enough to have precipitated a declaration of the Environmental Committee of the European Parliament to the effect that socio-economic factors be added to the criteria for judging new drugs (along with the existing criteria of safety, efficacy, and quality).

The socialist mentality is a tough nut for American business to crack as well. Despite a generally liberalized EC market place, a decades-old policy of government ownership or control of all essential industries has left an unmistakable bureaucratic imprint. A case in point: For twenty years there have been no sales of American heavy electrical equipment to EC member country utilities. According to the National Electrical Manufacturers Association, from 1975 to 1988, U.S. producers of large power transformers and steam turbines did not

The socialist mentality is a tough nut for American business to crack.

win a single order from an EC purchaser with a domestic production base for such products. Meanwhile, EC suppliers of such equipment represent 50 percent of the U.S. import market, which amounts to as much as 25 percent of the overall American market.

While the U.S. does have a "Buy American" policy for the TVA and BPA, about 50 percent of purchases in 1989 came from foreign sources (according to the Government Accounting Office). The EC directives pertaining to utilities allow oil and gas businesses to make special arrangements that can override public offers. Eighty percent of British sector North Sea procurement, for example, is sourced in the U.K.

The statistics show that only 10 to 15 percent of American companies export at all. Even fewer companies have the experience of operating in Europe as more than an exporter. The increasingly important service and non-price aspects of business are beyond the reach of a company serving a distant, new market through a representative, but unschooled, third party. The logical consequence of the completion of the Single Market is a likely reduction of U.S. exports to competitive markets. It has been suggested that "Lower costs and lower prices will improve the international competitiveness of European products and they may increase exports to non-EC countries. Simultaneously, there could be some shift from imported to domestic goods."[9]

Traditionally captive American markets may be threatened as well. In regions dominated by American exporters, the Single European Market will bring new competitors. According to chairman Candido Velasquez of Spain's Telefonica, "The big companies realize that with EC liberalization they will lose part of their markets, so they must seek new ones."[10] As Telefonica moves aggressively into Latin America, U.S. firms with significant market shares based on exports there will be the losers. Spanish banks also are implementing plans to move into Latin America to compensate for the loss of domestic business to larger EC banks. In fact, the Spanish government has a $12 billion plan in place to promote Latin American trade and joint ventures in Argentina, Chile, Mexico, Venezuela, and Brazil. There is much room for improvement. Spain conducted less than 5 percent of its trade with Latin America in 1989.

For those who would still insist that American companies prepare to participate fully and equally in Single Market Europe, the automobile industry should serve as a valuable lesson.

For some time, the European Commission has declared its intention to eliminate national VRA's and quotas and perhaps establish less rigorous ones at the EC level. The automotive industry—directly affected by such policies—gets more than the average amount of attention because of its employment base and comparatively low productivity. That the European automobile industry fears Japanese imports is manifest in quotas that limit imports to 3 percent in France (of a total annual market of nearly 2.5 million cars) and 1 percent in Italy. The Japanese market share represents nearly 40 percent of the Irish market where there are no such restrictions (Figure 9).

FIGURE 9:   1990 NEW CAR SALES
             EC MARKET SHARE

Volkswagen	15.5%
Fiat	15.0%
Peugot	13.0%
Ford	11.3%
GM	11.7%
Renault	10.2%
Mercedes	3.0%
BMW	2.9%
Toyota	2.6%
Nissan	2.7%
Mitsubishi	1.2%
Mazda	2.0%
Honda	1.0%
Other	7.9%
Total	**100.0%**

Source: European Commission, U.S. Dept. of Commerce

The EC has listened closely to the French who have demanded a Community-wide quota on Japanese cars that extends into the 21st century. The French also demand exceptions for even tighter limits in France and other individual markets. The Commission pressured to apply these quotas to Japanese cars built anywhere, whether in the Community or the U.S. Europeans have been pressed to back off of their original plan to limit Japanese imports to 9 percent of the 13.5 million car European market through 1997. Japan had tacitly agreed to separately limit the market share of its European-built cars as well.

Europeans point to Americans as having foolishly allowed American-built Japanese cars to take 20 percent of its market. This is an error Europeans vow to avoid.

So, while the door to export, acquisition, cultural acclimatization, and technological acceptance remains open, the strong wind of change may soon blow it shut. The pressures exerted on the European Commission by its member states with the end of the economic expansion will simply be the manifestations of a continent falling back on a centuries-old political heritage. The terrible economic drain of rebuilding Eastern Europe and the associated decline in the standard of living of Western Europeans will not be tolerated at the grass-roots level without the psychological crutch of trade protection.

It remains for American businesses to seize this window of opportunity before events beyond their control force it shut. By doing so, these firms will set a solid foundation for a future in the internal economy of the European Community.

II
EUROMARKETING

5

Complacency Invites European Competition at Home: Looking Back

C*orrectional Business Quarterly (CBQ):* John, given your entrepreneurial and managerial successes during your career, it is not surprising to see you caught up in the whirlwind of new business pursuits here in your new surroundings. Can you tell us what you found when you first arrived at N.I.D.P.?

John Technologue (JT): Well, as you know, my career has included the start-up, development, and management of businesses of all kinds, both technical and nontechnical. When I was brought to N.I.D.P., I was alarmed to see the basic management deficiencies that were present. On the other hand, I saw great opportunities for improvement, expansion, and profitability. There was an able workforce with an ample supply of technical, marketing, and financial skills. Our asset base was a bit thin, with most of our installed plant quite dated

43

but still functional. And, of course, raising capital would not be the problem it has often been for me in the past. The missing ingredient was motivation. My new colleagues desperately needed a goal to pursue, an end to achieve. And I became determined to give it to them.

CBQ: What were the big income earners at N.I.D.P. before you arrived, John, and how did you change that mix?

JT: The fact of the matter is, I didn't have to change the product mix too much at N.I.D.P. We already had some very strong, basic products with traditionally solid contractual relationships with our customers. For example, our automobile license plate line (LP) has been a standard in our region for years, and we have faithfully served our customers by keeping our prices down, despite the exceptionally high labor content of the product.

Nevertheless, I became concerned that too many of our eggs were being placed in one basket. There is no shortage of competition in the LP business, and there are new sources popping up all over the country. While researching the field, early in my tenure at N.I.D.P., I was shocked to learn that a growing percentage of the market was being wrested away from American producers by Western Europeans. Their highly automated production facilities and economies of scale, all implemented since the early 1990s, were digging deep into our market share. We were having to provide more service while working on lower margins just to maintain market share, let alone increase it.

As I saw it then, and I knew it from my own experience, we were going to have to beat the invaders at their own game. Western Europe was a growing market, one in which we had not even taken the first steps. Our distribution had always been taken for granted so our market strategy was embarrassingly simple. We did very little in the way of promotion or advertising, and our planning was minimal. A single staff person controlled all of our marketing activities.

No international role was identified, nor was an individual designated with like responsibilities.

CBQ: So, your strategy was market oriented rather than product oriented?

JT: Well, there was really very little done on either the product or market fronts since the limitations of our funding sources pretty much excluded any spending on research and development. Our customer relationships were so long-standing that marketing and strategic planning seemed superfluous.

FIGURE 10:   WEAKNESS ABROAD INVITES INVASION AT HOME
Production capacity in the U.S. owned by American companies

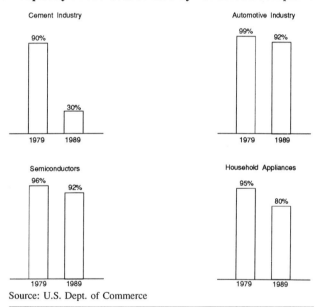

Source: U.S. Dept. of Commerce

CBQ: Why did you choose Europe as a target rather than markets closer to home? What about Texas or New York?

JT: If you take a look at the demographics, it becomes obvious that Texas and New York, to use your examples, are large LP markets. Yet these are mature markets served by an increasingly large group of competitors. For N.I.D.P., it made no sense to go after regional markets with additional competitors, some of whom were better staffed and better funded than we.

CBQ: John, I hope you don't mind if we extend the length of this interview. I think our readers will find this topic enormously interesting. Are we keeping you from anything?

JT: Please don't worry yourself about it. It's a pleasure at this point in my career to be able to say, "I have all the time in the world!"

CBQ: Well then, if not elsewhere in the U.S., why Europe? Why not Japan or Latin America?

JT: Well, in the case of Latin America, their labor costs were too low for us to be price competitive. At the same time, their economies are pretty unstable. Our arrangements here have locked us in to some very high direct labor costs, and, of course, just look around you and you can see that the benefits are extensive and costly.

I'd learned from my earlier experiences that Europe was a market to be reckoned with. We would have to get there if for no other reason than to save our product. With Europeans stealing market share here as quickly as they were, we were finding ourselves with excess capacity. We went looking for new markets, and this time, I had some serious market research done. We discovered that opportunities existed that we had never imagined. And these opportunities had the dual effect of expanding our sales and limiting the attention of our domestic European competition. They now had reason to be concerned about *their* home markets, and this distraction was enough to help us get back our momentum in the U.S.

CBQ: What had you learned at Diddley Technologies that could be applied at N.I.D.P.?

JT: Wasn't it clear? You read the post-mortems. At Diddley, we thought we owned the American market. When our grip started slipping in the late '80s we looked for new markets and discussed Europe in considerable detail. We hired consultants. We hired legal counsel in all twelve EC countries. And yet, we became convinced that the United States of Europe was going to be so exclusionary in its policies toward outsiders that it was pointless to invest in overcoming the substantial barriers to entry.

I won't make that mistake again. Here at N.I.D.P., we understand that expansion to Europe and protection of our domestic markets are integral parts of an overall market strategy. One hand washes the other. Shortly after I joined N.I.D.P., we engaged a trusted European agent to look for joint venture partners within the EC. Of course, I would have preferred to have carried out that search myself, but, as you know, the restrictions on travel here at N.I.D.P. are significant. We now have marketing agreements in place with two partners, one in Germany and the other in Spain, who not only distribute our products throughout their business territories, but who also supply us with our new designer-import line of license plates for distribution to our market base. This export portion of our business now contributes more than one-third of our sales and an even larger portion of our net income. Since our effective income tax rate is zero, a good deal of that earning power gets ploughed back into N.I.D.P. and makes life a little more comfortable for each of us here.

CBQ: Without going into any of the gory details, what happened at Diddley, and how could so successful and enterprise disappear overnight?

JT: It was really quite a classic business and psychological case study. Our failure to move into Europe encouraged our European competition to eat away at our American market share unthreatened by the possibility of a counter attack at home. With their own local markets secure, they were able to focus all their efforts on the American market. Soon they were hiring away our best sales people, and with them went our long standing customer relationships. Our shrinking earnings and cash flow limited our ability to reward our production staff and quality began to suffer. As managers bailed out, I was not only at my wits end, but I also was in unprecedented financial hot water. My wife hired a moving company to take my things and relocate me to a transient hotel in town. My children began denying any relationship to me. But that didn't stop them from demanding higher support payments. Finally, my chief financial officer hatched the embezzlement scheme that landed us both here at N.I.D.P.

CBQ: Have your superiors and peers here at N.I.D.P. accepted you as a functioning member of the team?

JT: Oh, I am very gratified at the support I have been given by both the warden and the other inmates. They have looked to me for guidance in turning the LP operation into a growing profit center and I believe that I have lived up to those expectations.

CBQ: John, I want to thank you for taking the time today to speak with CBQ. Success stories like yours make life tolerable for those who find themselves with unusual amounts of unstructured free time for an extended period of years.

JT: Thank you for coming all the way out to the Northern Illinois Debters' Prison to see me. Do you have to leave already? Why don't you stay for lunch? Let me show you around the grounds? There is a softball game scheduled for later this afternoon.....

6

A European Business and Strategy Overview

The Seven Rules of a Strategic Alliance

In the first quarter of 1990, 357 European companies were acquired by other European, American or Japanese organizations.[1] This became the fourth consecutive quarter during which the level of activity was far above that of earlier time periods. The details point to two interesting developments. First, American companies were involved in a decreasing number of these deals, and with a dramatically lower overall value (Figure 11).

Second, European and Japanese businesses are really forcing the consolidation of the Single Market. According to this data, companies from France and Germany initiated the greatest numbers of acquisitions—France alone accounted for almost fifteen percent of the deals in the quarter. And, while France was the leader in acquisitions abroad during the quarter, it

49

FIGURE 11:   INTERNATIONAL ACQUISITIONS IN EUROPE
(Mergers and acquisitions in EC by its largest 1,000 companies)

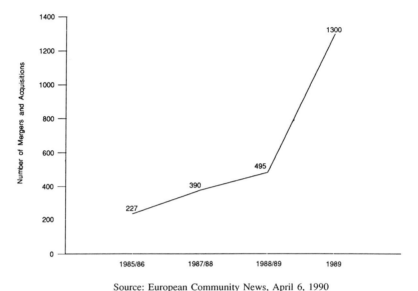

Source: European Community News, April 6, 1990

was also the leading target of acquirers (in value of companies acquired).

According to *Translink's European Deal Review*, the fact that American companies are slowing their rate of European acquisitions reflects a change in the American approach to the new Europe. Many of those American companies who were acquirers during this period were medium sized companies who were not likely to have already had much European activity.

In the summer of 1990, a survey of American companies with annual sales of between one and 200 million dollars was completed by the Market Access Europe Company (Brussels).[2] The survey focused on company attitudes toward the European Single Market.

Seventy percent of the managers surveyed stated that they did not have detailed information concerning EC projects or legislation affecting their markets. And, yet, 41 percent of these companies already had activities in Europe! One-third of the companies surveyed believed that a "Fortress Europe" was in the making, and only 19 percent believed that the American government was doing enough to protect American commercial interests in the Community. In addition, only 25 percent of the respondents felt that their own company actions in Europe were sufficient to protect and develop competitive positions there.

Where the largest companies were stepping back and solidifying their European operations, smaller companies were just getting started.

American multinationals established the pattern in the early and mid-1980s. They made their strategic acquisitions and began to rationalize some of their far-flung production and distribution. This explains the "non-event" tag that so many have placed next to "1992." For them, it is not a "New Europe" but an evolving market place in which the rules are, for the most part, simply mirroring their own actions and activities.

Industrial Consequences of the Single Market

What industries will be affected by the consolidation of the Single Market, and to what degree? While each industry will encounter a maze of new restrictions and freedoms, the relative benefit and potential gain is clearly greater for some.

The chart below (Figure 12) describes the relative impact of changes in six barriers to trade on over thirty industrial sectors (Figure 12).

For example, the food and drink industry is already a beneficiary of newly open borders and harmonized technical standards. The multinational nature of the business and the free movement of capital combine to offer new opportunities for cost savings and efficiencies. Mergers in the food processing industry seem to make great sense in the light of growing opportunities

FIGURE 12:   NEW EUROPE'S IMPACT ON INDUSTRY

Industries:	Suppression of border controls fisc. harm.	Techn. standards	Interventions & gov't contracts	Services & labor market	Circulation of capital & company law	EC R&D programs	General assessment
Food, drink & tobacco	XX	XX	X		X		•••
Energy	X	X	X		X		••
Steel			X		X		•
Metallurgy	X						−
Paper-cardboard		X					−
Glass							−
Chemicals					X	X	•
Plastics processing	X				X		•
Heavy mech. & elec. equip	X	X	XX		X	X	•••
Spec. mech. equip.		X			X		•
Precision & med. equip.		X	X		X	X	••
Data proc. equip.		X				XX	•
Telecoms equip.	X	XX	XX		X	XX	•••
Prof. electronics		X	X		X	XX	••
Household appliances					X		−
Consumer electronics	X	X			X	X	••
Automotive construction	XX	XX				X	•••
Aerospace construction		X	X		X	XX	••

	Suppression of border controls fisc. harm.	Techn. standards	Interventions & gov't contracts	Services & labor market	Circulation of capital & company law	EC R&D programs	General assessment
Industries:							
Pharmaceuticals	X	XX	XX		X	X	•••
Textiles-clothing-shoes	X				X		•
Furniture	X				X		•
Printing-publishing	X						–
Construction & Services							
Construction		X	X		XX		••
Air transportation			XX	XX	XX		•••
Other transportation			X	X	X		•
Telecoms services		X	XX	X	X	X	•••
Retail sales			X	X	X		•
Wholesales	X			X	XX		••
Professions			X	XX	X		••
Business services			X	X	XX	XX	•••
Banking	XX			XX	XX		•••
Insurance	XX			XX	XX		•••

Key   Nothing = little or no specific impact - X = a great impact - XX = a very great impact
An overall assessment has been obtained in addition to the ranking by each of these criteria
Key
  – = a score of 0 or 1   = little impact
  • = a score of 2 or 3   = a noticable impact
  ••• = a score of 4 or 5   = a great impact

Source: EC, Swiss Bank Corporation

for economies of scale across all of Europe—specifically to take advantage of markets that are now open to ingredient tests. In the paper industry, where consolidation proceeds and international giants, such as International Paper, continue to acquire positions within the Community, the greatest benefit seems to come from a relaxing of technical scrutiny by competing supervisory agencies. The overall effect of the Single Market is anything but neutral, and both the demographics and new economics of the market place make acquiring positions attractive.

In choosing just five of these industries, the chart below (Figure 13) describes six characteristic business activities on which the Single Market has its greatest impact.

While reduced trade barriers directly benefit the food, chemical, pharmaceutical, and auto industries, local content rules may reduce the potential benefit for the telecommunications industry. R&D costs will continue to demand ever-increasing investments, while simultaneous relief comes to participants in joint European projects. Decentralization of the R&D function, often necessary in playing the part of a good, pan-European corporate citizen, implies an increase in associated overhead. Ultimately, the strength of such a presentation of "impacts" is in its ability to point to the potential and needs for acquisition and joint venture in each of the five industries cited.

Joint Ventures, Partnerships, Mergers, Acquisitions

Single Market Europe developed momentum when large, multinational companies decided, for strategic reasons, that their presence in certain regional or niche markets had to grow. Many of these Single Market pioneers had the wherewithal to establish their own operations within the Community. Others were able to buy their way into the market place, and in doing so, acquire knowledge, staff, and a cultural affinity that the

FIGURE 13: THE NEW EUROPE DEMANDS STRATEGIC ALLIANCES

Impact \ Industry	Food and drink	Chemicals and Pharmaceuticals	Engineering and Plant Construction	Motor Vehicles	Telecommunication	Overall impact
Benefits from reduced trade barriers	+	+		+		+
Reduced R&D costs		+−	+−	+−		~
Price pressure		−+		+		+
Investment need	+	+	+	+	+	+
International presence	+	+	+	+	+	+
Acquisition and joint venture potential	+	+	+	+	+	+
Leading EC-companies	Unilever (NL) Nestlé (CH) Grand Metropolitan (GB) Allied Lyons (GB) BSN (F)	BASF (D) Bayer (D) Hoechst (D) ICI (GB) Ciba-Geigy (CH)	ABB (CH/S) MAN (D) Alsthom (F) Sulzer (CH) Hawker Siddeley (GB)	Daimler-Benz (D) Fiat (I) VW (D) Peugeot (F) Volvo (S)	Siemens (D) Ericsson (S) Alcatel (F)	

D= Germany
CH= Switzerland
GB= Great Britain
F= France
N= Netherlands
I= Italy
S= Sweden

Source: Swiss Bank Corporation

outsider takes some time to appreciate. Still others formed partnerships, alliances, and "enhanced" customer/supplier relationships.

Each of these joint ventures, partnerships and other common relationships can be called a "strategic alliance." What is a strategic alliance? It is a cooperative business relationship between two entities each of whom is going to give and take in order to capitalize on perceived product opportunities, cost savings, market penetration, and operating strategies. When, in suburban America, a video rental business allies itself with a chain of grocery stores to rent and sell video tapes to the public, each partner brings something to the party, and each benefits correspondingly. The grocery guarantees retail traffic, and the video business brings its operating expertise to bear in a booming consumer market segment.

Similarly, Bell Atlantic, one of the East Coast Bell Operating Companies, has network planning and management knowledge beyond that of most European PTT's. It knows the systems integration business. It is this expertise that Bell Atlantic brings to the table when it goes looking for partners in the telecommunications and information technology businesses in Europe.

In 1989, Bell Atlantic provided the Dutch PTT with a software system that helps the PTT forecast telephone network demand. In Madrid, Spain, Bell Atlantic helped install a system that apportions private line service. In addition to sales volume, Bell Atlantic is building an operating profile in a comparatively virgin market courtesy of the former market segment monopolists. The company has put together a five year business development plan for Europe largely based on developing "alliances" with those who might be thought of as both competitors and customers. From a standing start, Bell Atlantic now employs more than 700 in fifty one locations in eight European countries, with a headquarters, at the heart of the EC, in Brussels.

As one of the older, truly international businesses, the automobile industry has been taking advantage of strategic alliances and joint ventures for years. American innovation, Far Eastern production techniques and European styling and engineering have been combined in the products of most of the major manufacturers. The benefits of common research, marketing, or product sourcing is so apparent to most in the industry that Ferrari has an agreement with Fiat, who has an agreement with Nissan, who has an agreement with Fuji Heavy Industries, who has an agreement with Isuzu Motors, who has an agreement with General Motors, who has an agreement with Volvo! Volkswagen has an agreement with AutoLatina, who has an agreement with Ford Motor Company, who has an agreement with Mazda.[3]

Why have these large, multinationals traditionally pursued such strategic alliances, and to what end?

According to a classic study of the subject,[4] the traditional joint venture is a tool that has been used by global, development-intensive industries for some very specific reasons.

- Seventy five percent of joint venture agreements during the period studied took place in the aerospace, automobile, computer or telecommunications industries—all industries with high product development costs.

- Joint ventures among large companies have required global markets for a partner's products in order to justify such high development costs.

- Forty percent of these joint ventures focus exclusively on product development, specifically to spread the cost and financial risk of the R & D process.

- Because only 25 percent of the joint ventures studied involved marketing or production, it is understood that most of this strategic cooperation is not focused on the "bottom line." Rather than stake its future on this joint activity, each partner is hop-

ing for some marginal benefit from the cooperation.

- It is interesting to note that the Japanese use joint
ventures to produce, promote, and market products that have already been tested in the Japanese
domestic market. They use these cooperative activities specifically to help the bottom line. While
this gives the producer an opportunity to make
technical product improvements, it affords neither
the Japanese nor the Americans the opportunity to
exploit market strategies that are subject to cultural or language influence. It is for this reason
that the Japanese penetration of Europe has, until
quite recently, been limited to just a handful of
product categories.

The Strategic Decision

For most businesses, the expansion decision need not be
a difficult one.

What markets do you want to be in? What are you
successful with now? What are your strengths and areas
of expertise?

*Is there a sufficiently large market in each of
these areas now?* Have you done sufficient market
research or hired and expert to do so? Are your markets
of interest growing markets? Who and how strong are
your competi*tors?*

*Do you make or sell something for which there is
a market in Europe?* What are the economics and
possible economies of scale in European production?
Do these vary according to region? Will you be able to
find skilled employees in these regions?

*Do you understand technological trends in the
field?* How will they effect the development of the
market?

What are the financial requirements? Can you
fund this expansion without endangering your domestic

business? Are foreign sources of capital available, and at what price?

While the analysis of expansion potential is not the subject of this book, these basic questions need answers before expansion, and consequently, applicable strategies, can be considered. If Europe is already an attractive market, then the most significant consideration may be: Should I export or invest?

After having read the earlier portions of this book, the reader should be convinced that the economic and political uncertainties endemic to the development of the Single Market are not going to disappear. On the contrary, they will become more numerous as the Continent slips into recession or as the economic strain of rebuilding Eastern Europe takes its toll on the wallet of the rank and file West German worker.

The American Experience

The American experience is quite clear. When our industries are threatened by less expensive or by higher quality imports, a cry of despair goes up to Washington and protectionist legislation is imposed—Buy American! A late 1989 Harris Organization poll revealed that two-thirds of the American public agreed that the United States should take steps to discourage further Japanese investment in the country. The pressure on Europeans, with a history of tightly controlled economies, will be even greater, particularly in the face of an economic downturn. Remember, "Euro-phoria" began in the midst of the longest economic expansion in Western history.

In spite of the urgings of the U.S. Commerce Department to the contrary, it is more likely than not that our exports to Europe will be threatened in a variety of ways over the next several years. For the very short term, exporting may be an effective part of the expansion program—a technique of developing both market research and a product profile in various European markets. However, this is at best a part of a longer term strategy to invest in Europe in order to avoid business dislocations borne of Continental protectionism (Figure 14).

FIGURE 14:   RESTRICTIONS ON EC IMPORTS WILL DO MAJOR DAMAGE TO INTERNATIONAL TRADE
(The percentage of each country's overall exports that go to EC)

Country's exports that go to EC	Percentage
State-trading countries	14
Australia	15
Japan	18
USA	24
LDC	24
OPEC	32
Yugoslavia	37
Turkey	44
Finland	44
Sweden	52
Switzerland	56
Austria	64
Norway	65

Source: Globus, 1989, Swiss Bank Corporation

Oracle Corporation, now the dominant software company in Europe, began its foray there by exporting to local distributors. After learning its way around the market place, it bought out its distributors and set up its own offices in major export markets. Just making that extra commitment to the local markets caused an immediate jump in the level of European sales.

What, then, are the investment alternatives?

1. Do you invest in building an asset base or market presence from scratch?

2. Should you buy your asset base or market presence by making an acquisition?

3. Or, should you look for a partner with whose cooperation investment can be minimized while you learn
about the market?

Most companies are simply not willing to accept
the risk associated with the first two alternatives. If you
are not already a well researched expert on the target
markets, then the process of building from scratch will
in itself be a trip up the learning curve—and an expensive one at that. Mistakes may stay with you too, like a
badly tailored Italian suit, coloring your products or
services in the market well after they no longer are
representative of your activities.

Acquisition gets you into the market, often in a big
way, but are you in the best position to do the due
diligence necessary to insure that your acquisition target
is everything it seems to be? Managers at the Wallace,
Smith Trust Company Ltd. (U.K.) estimate that there are
twenty five companies who are prospective buyers for
each firm that wants to sell. It is not surprising, then, to
hear that that nearly three-quarters of such corporate
acquisitions are considered failures by the buyers. Remember, in the Single Market, you are the foreigner—
from a different culture and with a different financial
system and sense of fiscal responsibility. So, after all is
said and done, it just plain makes sense to get your feet
wet in someone else's pool. Live and learn.

The Business "Starter-Kit"

Think of strategic partnerships and alliances as starter
kits—something you can build on, and if necessary, get
out of later, when you and your partner have grown in
different strategic directions. Or, think of it as more of
an engagement and less of a marriage. On the other
hand, some alliances last a good long time, bringing
benefit to each partner in great and nearly equal measure. For the most part, however, Europeans have allied
with American companies in order to acquire key tech-

nologies, while the American partner is looking for market knowledge and cultural entree.

Benefits of Strategic Alliance

1. RAPID MARKET ENTRY
2. ACQUIRE EXPERTISE & COMPE-
    TENCE MORE CHEAPLY THAN
    THROUGH PURCHASE
3. REDUCE POLITICAL RISKS
4. . SHARE ECONOMIC RISKS

Anadigics (New Jersey) makes gallium arsenide integrated circuits.[5] With so new a technology, the company was forced to think globally. In trying to attract interest for its technology, the company put on its own private trade shows all over Europe. It was able to promote a new application in consumer electronics to a European industry hungry for any advantage with which it could counter the Japanese. By presenting itself as a non-Japanese supplier of chips in its seminars, Anadigics was able to attract equity investments from Thomson-CFS and N.V. Philips, each of whom wanted to guarantee its supply of chip production.

There are a number of opportunities being provided by the Department of Commerce and by trade associations to strut your stuff before your European market niche. You can also request information on every major trade show and exhibition in Europe and be a welcomed visitor or exhibitor.

Suppose, for example, that you are a snack food distributor who has covered the U.S. with your new, all-natural candy bar. You are looking for new markets. Upon hearing that your state association trade representative is going to attend a trade show in France, you send along a supply of samples with some literature. At the show, which you do not attend, and in fact, have forgotten all about, your state representative passes out thousands of your samples and returns with a list of interested European distributors and even a couple of manufacturers. Over the next six months, you negotiate an agreement to export 1,000 cases of your product to a confectionery/manufacturing company in Belgium, giving him a great price and relinquishing complete marketing responsibility to him. You gain early entry to the nascent EC healthy snack market and you lock into existing distribution. However, you do lose a great deal of control of your marketing in Europe, but you are getting large orders and have held out the possibility of renegotiating the contract down the road once you've increased your European knowledge base.

You needn't feel that such arrangements apply only to smaller domestic companies either. Coca Cola has joint ventured with Cadbury Schweppes in the U.K. in order to take advantage of an existing European marketing and distribution system. And it had quite a valuable product franchise to share in return.

American trade associations are working hard to push member companies into international markets. The American Electronics Association is vigorously encouraging its members to form alliances, where possible, with European partners in order to protect and expand market positions in the face of the completion of the Single Market. But Richard Iverson, AEA president, has encouraged his constituents to get the agreement clear on paper—even to the degree of inviting an independent third party to attend negotiations in order to be sure that all salient points are covered and all strategy angles are both compatible and protected.

In the early 1980s a study of corporate joint ventures[6] found that the participants described only 42 percent of them as good and 22 percent as satisfactory, while 36 percent were described as unsatisfactory. Responsibility for the failed alliance could usually be assigned to the irrepressible need of one or both partners to assert his manhood. In a joint venture, either one partner is the boss, neither is the boss, or both share the role equally. When an agreement establishes one partner as dominant, then the venture can proceed in one of two ways—unencumbered or with an overbearing level of intrusion. If each partner must control 50 percent of the activity, then, more often than not, the partnership will be short-lived.

According to research by I.J. Reynolds,[7] about one-half of joint ventures fail, usually due to conflicts between owners of the joint enterprise. Killing found, in fact, that those ventures run with independent managements had the highest chances for success, while those with joint management had the highest failure rates.

Working out a Strategic Alliance: Seven Rules to Live By

FIGURE 15:   SEVEN RULES TO LIVE BY IN BUILDING A STRATEGIC ALLIANCE

1.   List your objectives and list those of your ally.

2.   Try to get a handle on any potential for conflict between the two (or more) of you.

3.   What will each partner contribute to the venture?

4.   Measure your partner.

5.   What happens when one partner wants out?

6.   Don't overburden the alliance with management control and reporting systems.

7.   Conclude negotiations with an ironclad legal aggreement.

Suppose you were actually to find a potential ally in the target market. How would you put together a working arrangement?

1. *List your objectives and list those of your ally.* How do these lists match up? Are they complementary or are they in conflict? Does either party require that the venture be profitable in the very short term? There could be political or administrative reasons for this. If, however, one or both partners will pressure the venture to turn over profits in order to justify its existence, it will bleed to death. Be sure that both you and your prospective partner can afford to let the venture develop and grow.

2. *Try to get a handle on any potential for conflict between you and your ally.* How much information will you be sharing? If your proprietary information is key to making the arrangement work, how much are you willing to share? If you are not willing to share the key information, then can you really hope to benefit from such an arrangement? It is often better to make the up-front assumption that your new partner, in the course of the venture, will learn all of your proprietary secrets. Accept that and write the cost of that information into your agreement. You must either sell it going in or keep it a totally separate issue.

3. *What will each partner contribute to the venture?* The European partner may be looking for technology transfer. Nevertheless, look for other things that you can bring to the table that will build the value of your case. Can you offer management expertise, cash, or perhaps reciprocal marketing arrangements for his products in the U.S.? Each of these gives you grounds to ask for a bigger piece of the pie.

4. *Measure your partner.* What kind of alliance makes sense? Will you share responsibility and operation equally, or will the alliance result in a new entity with joint ownership? Will the language of your agreement restrain the alliance in a detrimental way, or will the venture be free to pursue the goals for which it has been designed?

5. *What happens when one of you wants out?* How can this alliance be dissolved? Be sure to know who will own what—particularly as regards any proprietary information or technology, either contributed by one of the partners or developed jointly.

6. *Don't overburden your alliance with management control and reporting systems.* In his "Organization of International Joint Ventures," (Conference Board Report #787, New York, 1980) Janger studied the management control systems of 168 joint ventures and found that quantitative control of the ventures was monitored with extensive financial reporting and auditing. In addition, staff performance was monitored closely and audited frequently. *Step back for a minute.* One of the benefits of your joint activities will be the creative flow generated by the joining of two business cultures. So after having put things in place, be sure to let the creative juices flow. Don't strangle the operation with more than the necessary amount of reporting and auditing. There will be time for that later, once you are well on your way up the learning curve. Be willing to put up with a strong, decentralized organization that gives decision-making authority to regional groups. The Japanese have yet to learn how to place operations in the trust and control of Europeans and have limited their success as a result.

7. *Be sure that you conclude your negotiations with an understandable, ironclad legal agreement.* Leave no area to trust or doubt. You are operating in an environment that looks very American at times, but is based on a very different pattern of thought and structure of priorities. Areas that might be glossed over or dismissed as insignificant could return to haunt you and make the duration of the alliance intolerable for one or the other of the partners. Make no assumptions regarding commissions, termination of sales representative contracts, non-compete agreements, employee benefits, management contracts, or

copyright ownership. Scrutinize every area of possible contention.

Do you know, for example, that terminating a sales representative in Europe is nearly the equivalent of "buying him out" of his business? Do you know that overseas plaintiffs often sue American companies for actions that originate outside of the U.S.? The only way to protect yourself from liability may be to organize the joint venture as an independent corporation. On the other hand, the Supreme Court of Texas said it was all right to sue Union Carbide for its Bhopal, India, gas leak as long as there was some connection between the companies (legal term: nexus). Just supplying money or machinery to a venture might be enough. There may also be long-term environmental liabilities.

One Company's Experience

Exxel Container, Inc.[8] developed a new aerosol technology in the late 1980s. Seeing consumer packaging as a global business, Exxel developed a strategy that would support the customers of multinational companies without geographic limitations. Exxel began looking for partners with the ability to contribute both equity and distribution. The company, in effect, used the process of raising capital as its internationalization strategy.

In order to avoid a piecemeal partnership approach, Exxel looked for a single pan-European partner whose geographic coverage would be complete. Exxel began the process by hiring an individual in Europe as its representative to open discussions with potential partners. The individual chosen had already spent a career developing special relationships with executives in the packaging and related industries. (A retired executive or career trade organization man could be perfect for such a role and find a substantial equity, commission or royalty incentive quite attractive).

Although Exxel was dealing with a new technology, it chose to approach companies in their sales and marketing areas. By demonstrating the sales potential of the package, the company was able to excite prospective partners.

Exxel eventually settled on an agreement with AMS (a pan-European subsidiary of CMB Packaging) and gave up exclusive distribution rights. The company is also pursuing a manufacturing joint venture in order to take advantage of a home country location within the Single Market.

7

EuroMarketing: Some Differences in Approach

Two close friends, John and Bill, were chatting over a cup of coffee early one weekday morning. John, perhaps the most successful automobile salesman in the region, was on his way to his downtown showroom. Bill, his neighbor and commuting companion, was the marketing manager for a line of women's outerwear.

Each, convinced of the power of his business discipline, argued its merits. John made it painfully clear that Bill's carefully planned and customer-sensitive approach would be no match for his hard-driving, personal selling techniques in a one-on-one contest. After much give and take, the two agreed to put theory to the test. That day, during the lunch hour, they would each approach twenty passersby at a busy downtown street corner. Bill, the professional marketer, would offer each of his candidates a $5 bill in exchange for a $10 bill. John would offer each of his candidates a $10 bill in exchange for a $5 bill. The one returning with the greatest number of sales would be obligated to buy the other's lunch for the next month.

While convinced of the power of his approach, Bill was still astonished at the results. Six of his candidates actually "bought" his $5 bill for $10, while only three of John's candidates purchased his $10 bills for $5. At the end of each transaction, each candidate was questioned about his motivation. Each of those who traded down had been convinced of Bill's sincerity and strongly believed that it was the right thing to do. Those who would not take the obviously favorable exchange from John resented his manipulative sales techniques.

The Ugly American

Europeans often identify the technique employed by John as typically American. The hard sell is something that ordinary Europeans resent, and, the fact that they associate it with all things American simply presents another barrier to be overcome by American businesses operating in Europe.

The European approach to business is generally more formal and standoffish than the American approach. Familiarity breeds contentment. Europeans want to get to know you, and as a consequence, they want to get to know and trust your product or service. *Comfort, knowledge and trust will come before any business—particularly if a local alternative is available.*

On the other hand, European companies typically react to market changes more slowly than do American companies. A strong analogy can be drawn between the large, bureaucratic American company and the typical European commercial enterprise—Europeans are top-heavy with centralized management responsibility. Few decisions are made quickly, without the full consideration of several layers of management. This presents the more mobile, less bureaucratic American enterprise with a real advantage.

Then too, Bill, in the anecdote above, banked on his ability to read the market, that is, to be market-driven. A sales-driven company is a product-driven company. This also characterizes the European firm. For many years, Europe has taken pride in its finely tuned, highly engineered products. To a large extent, Western European manufacturers (Germans in particular) have convinced the market place that improvements in quality vastly out weigh all other purchasing decision factors. They have learned to force their high quality merchandise on an accepting consumer.

Just as Europeans have become more international in perspective, they have now become more market-driven. They are first finding market opportunities and are then seeking to develop products and services to fill those niches. Historically market-driven American companies, particularly those with more entrepreneurial fervor, have a monetary advantage in this regard.

Modifying American Marketing Tools for European Markets

Expansion-related objectives require the transfer and modification of strategic marketing tools for use in the European market place. With that in mind, a brief review of some basic principles of *market gap analysis* is called for (Figure 16).

Market gap analysis is little more than a common sense way to structure one's approach to the selection of a market and product niche. In general, this is a

---

FIGURE 16:   MARKET GAP ANALYSIS

1. Identify Company Objectives
2. Segment the Target Industry
3. Problems and Needs Assessment for Target Markets
4. Identify and Confirm Market Gaps
5. Market Research and Analysis

five-step process that, while intimidating in appearance, orders one's thought and approach and, in the end, pinpoints the target niche.

The analysis begins with the *identification of company objectives:*

1. What industry do you want to address? With so much industry overlap, you must be specific.

2. What kind of product or service do you want to offer to this industry? Is it a high-technology product or a low-tech product? Is it electronic or mechanical? Is it a highly customized or engineered product or one that lends itself well to outside contracting?

3. Is there a profit or margin criteria that you must meet? Based on that, what is the minimum market potential that your efforts will need to satisfy?

4. What level of competition are you willing to encounter? Do you have to be one of the first in the market with such a product or can it be an already well developed marketplace with many competitors?

5. Is this to be a pioneering effort on your part? Do you want to introduce a new product and invest in its promotion or do you want to build on an existing market profile, saving yourself the cost of trailblazing?

6. Do you want to set up your own sales distribution network or use an existing network?

7. Is the idea to transfer some American knowledge, expertise or experience, or to develop entirely new products, services, or techniques?

Once having set the objectives, *the next step is to break down the industry in question into segments.* Classic market analysis usually defines the nature of potential market segments in one of three ways:

1. Geographic—by region, urban or rural, by climate

2. Demographic—by age, sex, family size, income, education, religion, race, etc.

3. Psychographic—by lifestyle or personality traits

European market segmentation can get a bit muddled. If you choose to segment the market geographically, for example, why limit yourself to just Germany, when the language and culture of all or parts of Austria and Switzerland are nearly identical? Or, if you choose a market based on demographics, will language and cultural differences limit your operating territory to too small a geographic region?

Once you have chosen several market segments, a *list of problems and needs is compiled for each of the target markets.* Remember, as a market-driven vendor, you are out to satisfy the needs and problems of your chosen market segment.

Now, *how many of those needs and problems conform to the criteria and objectives that you defined in the first step above?* Use this approach to narrow your choices further.

You now must choose among the market "gaps" that are left. But, before you can begin to formulate and implement a marketing program, you must *confirm these gaps.* Do they exist? How big are they? Your definition of the gap is now specific enough to lend itself well to both informal and formal market research.

Market research and analysis of your chosen niche can be done by professionals who specialize in this field, or in-house. If you are already located in Europe, the in-house process may not be as daunting as it appears. Through informal interviews you can accumulate a good deal of information. However, library research and discussions with Europe's very powerful trade associations will yield even more information than would a comparable American exercise. Europe has a collegial history and its commercial enterprises generally share more information than do their American counterparts.

The European Selling Process

The European selling process differs from the American process in certain respects. There is the cultural bias discussed earlier. In addition, there exists an ability to utilize trade shows and press releases to an even greater degree than in the U.S. Trade shows have been around in Europe since before American independence. Europe has several huge trade show centers that dwarf even America's largest. Participation in such a show as an exhibitor, or just as a visitor, promises many times the degree of exposure that one would expect from an American trade show. Whether you choose to go it alone or to use the Commerce Department's group alternative is another issue.

The disparate European press offers a variety of publications in many different languages. It is worth the effort to make your press releases available in every European language and to distribute them in many geographic markets.

Building a sales network in Europe differs only slightly from doing the same in the U.S. Just as in the U.S., it may take three years to build up a competent European sales force, particularly keeping in mind a sensitivity to different languages and cultures. *It may take only six months to put together and train a strong network of sales representatives.* The candidates can be evaluated by contacting customers (distributors, retailers, agencies), and they can be motivated in suspiciously American ways, by using merchandise, trips, and bonuses. Europeans also may be more susceptible to awards and other "ego builders" than are Americans. In the U.S., independent sales reps know that they will be terminated if they do poorly, and they know they will be terminated if they perform too well. In Europe, the motivation to perform well is less likely to be curbed by the buy out arrangement required in every representative's termination agreement. You cannot simply drop a European sales rep. You must actually "buy" his business (in your own product!) from him. This is actually a performance enhancement incentive for him.

As in any good sales setting, American firms should be hoping for objections from their customer candidates in Europe. Only objections will give outsiders a chance to offer their competitive advantage, differentiate themselves from other firms, and overcome sales hurdles. You will know that the European sitting across the table from you is not interested when your meeting is filled with smiles, agreement, and polite replies. Europeans will be cordial even if they have no interest in your offer.

Looking at European Industries

The face of European industry is changing quickly. In some cases, this change is being initiated by legislation. In others, the new competition among intra-European companies is creating a series of market opportunities in formerly mundane, slow-growth fields. The following section provides overviews of several European markets, notes opportunity where it exists, and points out legislation of concern. While providing a minimum of market detail, this section should give the reader a sense of the change that the Single Market has created in what were formerly closed, stagnating, or slowly growing segments.

The European Transportation Industry

Would you do business in a transportation market place where administrative delays account for as much as 40% of ground freight delivery schedules? According to Roger Kallock of Cleveland Consulting Associates,[1] a typical 1200 kilometer overland cargo trip within the United Kingdom took about thirty six hours in the late 1980s. An equivalent haul between London and Milan,

Italy took fifty eight hours, resulting in a fifty percent increase in the cost of transportation.

Even in the face of labor unrest and fifty separate regulatory systems, it has been some time since the American freight market was so inefficient. When compared to the rest of the world, North America is borderless.

Recognizing the futility of trying to develop a single market while maintaining separate customs and administrative documentation, the EC was quick to rally support in the mid-80s for the Single Administrative Document. The SAD has shortened intra-EC transit time and dramatically increased freight traffic efficiency.

The European trucking market traditionally has been closed to external competition. *The 1990 EC cabotage directive is allowing trucking firms from other member states as well as from the U.S. to participate in these previously closed shipping markets.* While 15,000 licenses will be issued by the EC monthly, local markets are likely to be left in local hands. Each license is a two month permit for a single vehicle to undertake cabotage. While 15,000 seems to be quite a significant number, it is subdivided among the twelve member states. "Full cabotage" is targeted for January of 1993, but the process is likely to proceed more slowly (Figure 17). The 15,000 licenses represent less than 10 percent of the EC cabotage market. Licensing power is being left in the hands of national authorities—which leaves many of the intangible trade barriers in place. While the invocation of reciprocity has been laid to rest, there is the lingering prejudice against carriers whose home countries do not offer such cabotage rights. Protection of local markets will continue to be asserted for some time by governments protecting well organized trucking lobbies. The 1990 German road tax on large trucks brought Germany into the European Court of Justice for imposing a non-tariff barrier to inter-Community trade. While the EC appears to have won this skirmish, it will be forced to deal with many more in the years to come.

**FIGURE 17:   EC MEMBER STATE TRANSPORTATION
PREFERENCES**

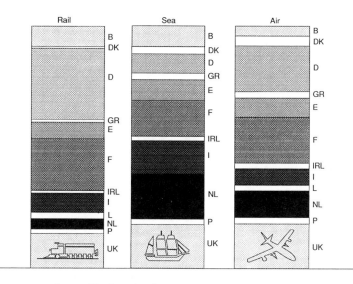

Source: The Jerusalem Post

Inter-Community trucking deregulation is proceeding by increasing the number of cross-border permits by 40 percent in 1991 and again by 40 percent in 1992.

An integrated European transportation market can offer American companies a path of entry and remove some logistic impediments as well. *The EC has put in place an "action program" that includes a variety of infrastructure improvements* among which is the construction of a high-speed rail line linking Paris, London, Amsterdam, and Cologne.

Other improvements include the modernization of the North-South inland waterway from The Netherlands to Belgium and France, and the upgrading of Alpine transit routes to Italy. Such large scale projects are bound to receive the continuing attention and funding of the European Commission. For American companies which have either not operated in Europe or who have been limited by its infrastructure, the future promises more efficient logistics and somewhat easier access.

Airline deregulation is also coming to Europe—perhaps not on the scale that we find common in North America, but on a sufficiently market-oriented basis to upset nearly every European national carrier.

Bi-lateral agreements and country-by-country subsidies of national carriers have guaranteed that the European aviation system have the highest passenger per mile fare structure in the developed world. The creation of the airline deregulation directive in the late '80s introduced the fear of American-style price wars into the hearts of each carrier. Member states have agreed to allow greater freedom for airlines to offer lower fares, apply these reforms to more European airports, and allow more freedom to pick up and drop off passengers in one EC country before transporting them to a third.

While some freedom to undercut official fares does exist, monopolistic habits die hard. For example, Air France purchased its competitor, L'Union des Transports Aeriens (UTA), as well as the domestic carrier, Air Inter, giving it 97 percent of the French airline industry. While the EC antitrust office objected to the UTA merger, close government ties and the support of Mr. Delors in Brussels carried the day.

*Other national carriers have moved quickly to strengthen themselves in the face of expected interna-*tional competition. A joint venture of British Airways, KLM (The Netherlands), and Sabena (Sweden) is designed to crowd out foreign carriers and lock up access to Brussels. Lufthansa is investing ten billion marks to upgrade and expand its 200 plane fleet by adding sixty-six more planes between 1990 and 1992. It also has purchased 26 percent of the East German carrier, Interflug, and will build a new hub in Berlin. Swissair is extending its reach and has purchased parts of both Delta and Singapore Airlines.

Nevertheless, regulation clearly protects the national carriers from external competition. EC fares are subject to a "double disapproval procedure." This means that the governments of both the country of arrival and the country of departure need to object to a proposed fare in order to reject it. Third-country carriers (read: U.S.) are specifically excluded from initiating new fares leaving such carriers at a considerable marketing disadvantage. In addition, European carriers can use their computerized reservation systems to discriminate against third-country vendors and carriers when the European Commission decides that a third country's system does not provide "equivalent, reciprocal treatment" for EC carriers. American system displays do not generally offer such reciprocal coverage.

If the European Community eventually negotiates its civil aviation agreements as a block rather than on a country-by-country, bilateral basis, third-country carriers might be interpreted to be in violation of cabotage regulations. There is also the possibility that the EC may wish to negotiate route rights with third-countries and their carriers. In doing so, they may demand reciprocal access to American markets, for example—a right they do not currently have. How will American carriers respond to the threat of additional domestic competition?

Suffice it to say that while the regulatory environment is nothing like the comparatively free transportation market system in place in the U.S., opportunities for American participation in Europe have been enhanced. *Where there was once effectively no opportunity for participation, there is now limited opportunity to participate and to use, on a limited basis, some of the strategies that have proved successful in the U.S.*

American Airlines has gone aggressively into Europe, both to get a foothold before the completion of the Single Market and because of the greater growth it sees there.[2] While air traffic in the U.S. is expected to grow at less than 4 percent annually, European growth is expected to be closer to 7 percent. There is already a great deal of European airport congestion so getting in position there now is essential.

American is capitalizing on the congestion at major U.S. and European airports to attract passengers from smaller markets and secondary hubs to feed its more fuel efficient, smaller planes. The company has emphasized service and cultural sensitivity in order to compete with the European carriers. At the same time, American has avoided the equity links that some other American airlines have forged with European carriers for fear that such arrangements could tie its hands in Europe.

Deregulation in the air cargo market is running quite a bit behind that of either ground transport or air passenger transport. In early 1990, the European Commission proposed lifting some restrictions on market entry and the setting of cargo rates. However, as proposed, the directive would retain a "genuine community link" component, limiting the right to provide some services to only those carriers who have their head offices and majority ownership in the EC.

It is just this sort of provision that was forced out of the original trucking cabotage directive. Its inclusion in the air cargo directive spells trouble for the many companies already operating in the European market. Should corporate pressures be sufficient to eliminate this provision, air cargo companies may well operate in Europe in much the same way as they already do in the U.S. and elsewhere.

The European Telecommunications Industry

It makes perfect sense that the European industries offering the greatest growth opportunities are also the best protected. While the European Commission has deregulated the telecommunications industry, exposing local PTT's to competition from the industries of their neighboring member-states, an added layer of protection has been imposed on the market through directives that force bids from companies outside of the EC to be viewed differently from those of their EC competitors.

As one of the four "protected sectors," telecommunications is perceived to be essential to the ultimate growth and survival of the European economy, both on a local and continental basis. In much the same way that the U.S. government has protected its telephone industry, Europe seeks to guarantee the growth of its own. At the same time, the EC wants to make the reconstruction and development of its continental communications systems more efficient and cost effective.

The language of the EC's telecommunication directives is just imprecise enough to allow member-state governments the leeway to interpret them to the benefit of the local PTT. *The telecommunication directives are likely to retain their 50 percent rule as well—a rule which elegantly combines local content and community preferences.* What's more, all equipment purchases of $500,000 or more are covered (read: transmission and switching equipment).

The American telecommunications industry is, to some extent, hostage to the political negotiating process that characterizes the GATT. Europe is willing to give up the 50 percent rule in trade. The EC wants the American Bell companies and AT&T to be covered by the GATT government procurement code. The U.S. negotiators state simply that these are private companies and therefore not subject to U.S. government dictates. Europeans claim that only 18 percent of the total U.S. telecommunications market consists of imports, and that only 5 percent of the central office market and 13 percent of the transmission market are imports. Europeans supply only 4 percent of American imports of transmission equipment, and the very process of becoming an approved Baby Bell vendor is, they claim, long and costly. The EC is willing to let GATT cover both its private and public operators (about twenty-five companies, including British Telecom), and asks that the U.S. do the same.

Until recently, continental telecommunications projects were the exclusive domain of local suppliers. *The $78 billion European Community telecommunica-*

tions market (1989) is now open to cross border competitive bidding. In the late 1980s, PTT's bought as much as 80 percent of the telecommunication equipment sold in many EC countries. The market is expected to grow to $104 billion by 1992—25 percent of the world market. Dataquest has projected European market growth of 8.5 percent annually through 1993, with revenues from services of $100 billion and nearly $30 billion from equipment.

On-site customer equipment (telephones, fax machines, telexes) amount to 24 percent of the EC equipment market, with transmission equipment equal to 13 percent. The numbers of digital lines to be installed annually in Europe is expected to grow at four times the rate of the U.S. into the early 1990s[3] (Figure 18 and 19).

While the data communications segment represents only 10 percent of the overall market, it is growing at a rate of 25 percent per year.[4]

France is particularly interested in the data services segment of the market. In fact, the French have consistently opposed opening the market for basic data services to external competition. In order to avoid "cream skimming" of basic services by private providers, the French have insisted on a program for licensing private operators, an approach opposed by the British, Dutch, Danish, and Germans.

Of course, unlike its sister states, France already operates a profitable, state-run videotext system (Minitel) which stands to be the big loser in a data services free-for-all.

The EC's Open Network Provision promises to give private operators access to all member state networks by providing a framework for harmonizing the conditions of their use, tariffs, and technical interfaces. The ONP directive not only moves toward harmonizing rules regarding the use of public networks for electronic mail, trading, and the like, it also sets out the rules for future directives on the specifics of leased lines, package and circuit-switched data services, integrated services

FIGURE 18:   THE EUROPEAN TELECOMMUNICATIONS MARKET (A)

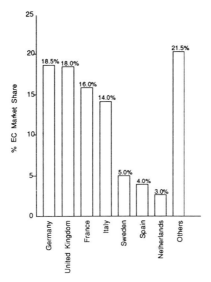

Source: Rmark Research, U.S. Department of Commerce

digital network (ISDN), telephone, broadband network services, and mobile phone services (Figure 20).

The EC Service Directive calls for free competition in value-added services by 1993 in the areas of electronic data interchange, electronic mail, and related services. According to the New York market research firm of Frost & Sullivan, *the value-added services market in the EC was $4.9 billion in 1989 and will grow to $15.9 billion by 1994.* The major American players in the market at the moment are General Electric, IBM, Telenet Communications Corporation and Infonet Services. General Electric has a private network niche, operating GE Information Services, a manager of private data networks in Europe. But, even with this newly legislated pan-European freedom, the host PTT's still can seek to restrict market entry by raising the cost of compliance in order to provide interconnection on leased lines.

FIGURE 19:   THE EUROPEAN TELECOMMUNICATIONS MARKET (B) (EQUIPMENT AND SERVICES)

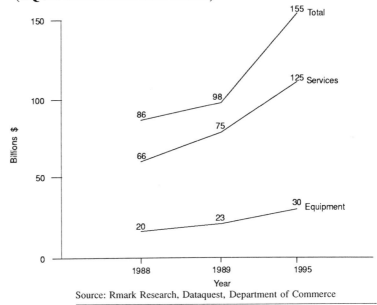

Source: Rmark Research, Dataquest, Department of Commerce

The terminal equipment directive contains a reciprocity provision that relates access to the EC market to comparable access by EC vendors to foreign markets. American markets are likely to look very open to the EC's vendors, leaving American manufacturers free to bid on European contracts within the confines of the "buy Europe," 50 percent rule which the services directive includes.

Just how big is the European telecommunications industry? It represents 3 percent of the gross domestic product of the European Community and is expected to reach 7 percent of its GDP by the year 2000. According to the European Commission, 60 percent of Europe's jobs are linked directly or indirectly to this industry.

With so much at stake, European businessmen and bureaucrats have privately been extremely critical of the American decision to open its own telecommunications markets to foreign providers without first making pro-

FIGURE 20:   EUROPEAN TELECOMMUNICATIONS TRANSMISSION EQUIPMENT MARKET SIZE

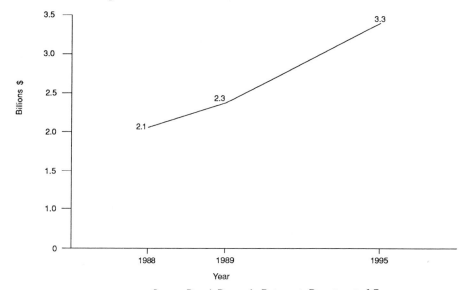

Source: Rmark Research, Dataquest, Department of Commerce

visions to protect itself. In the wake of that decision, the U.S. has been overwhelmed by imports, dumped goods, and predatory pricing, without having secured reciprocal market access for its domestic producers. However, it may be just this experience that will prepare the survivors of this American competition to succeed where the comparatively fat and complacent Europeans fail.

Slimmed down and tested American companies and technologies are already having an effect on the market. While AT&T has developed a successful European partnership and joint-venture strategy (In 1990, it joined Ericsson and Alcatel in order to supply a large Telefonica-Spain telephone equipment order), GenRad is promoting itself as "the Pan-European Telecommunications Specialist," while Teradyne has performed ISDN (Integrated Services Digital Network) testing for Siemens on its series 8500 testers. Innovative technologies and tested market niche strategies will dictate American success in the huge but wary European market.

The European Semiconductor Industry

Of the ten leading semiconductor companies in Europe, four are American, and three are Japanese. Only Philips, Siemens, and SGS-Thomson are European based. Europe controls only $8.8 billion of the $50 billion world semiconductor market. *In 1988, Europe's share of world chip output was only 10 percent and falling.*[5] European producers had only 7 percent of the U.S. chip market.

As the weak sister of the international semiconductor triumvirate, Europe has adopted a drastic strategy designed to retain and build market share in the face of North American and Far Eastern aggression. A variety of EC initiatives are aimed at jump starting the European technological development process. JESSI (see the EUROSPEAK appendix) has supported the R&D efforts of large and small European companies alike. JEMI, the Joint Equipment Manufacturers Initiative, brought thirty companies together in a cooperative venture designed to generate business for French semiconductor firms. Each has aspirations of supplying its product to international chip companies. Large semiconductor firms have become associate members of JEMI and are signing cooperative agreements with its members.

The EC is fighting hard to protect its native industry. In 1989, a directive covering semiconductor rules of origin was issued by the European Commission. As a result of the requirement that a substantial part of the chip's manufacture be done in Europe, a forced-investment explosion has taken place.

A proposed origin rule was to have considered only printed circuit boards with at least 45 percent European content as local, but in mid-1990 a stay of execution was given. Should the EC decide to go ahead and implement the rule, it is likely that "designing-out" of non-EC components will increase dramatically. Semiconductors and ICs that are shipped to the EC are subject to a 14 percent external tariff. On top of that, the 1989 semiconductor directive credits EC origin only to semiconductors which are "diffused" in the EC—all in the name of giving EC semiconductor manufacturers the breathing room needed to catch up to American and Japanese designers and producers.

In the face of such legislation, maintenance of European market share and hoped for growth has inspired both American and Japanese manufacturers to invest in the construction of European capacity. Intel quickly set about building a $450 million plant in Ireland. Fujitsu and Mitsubishi announced $650 and $300 million facilities in Great Britain and Germany respectively.

Under pressure from European manufacturers seeking price protection, the EC concluded an agreement with Japanese semiconductor manufacturers in 1990 on floor pricing of semiconductors. The EC was acting to protect its DRAM industry against eleven Japanese competitors who had been selling their chips in Europe at prices between 8.5 percent and 206 percent below the typical delivered DRAM price. Such practices had allowed the Japanese to increase their European market share from 24.6 percent in 1983 to 70.5 percent in 1987.[6] With prices never showing a differential of more than 2 percent from one vendor to another, it became clear to the EC that the Japanese suppliers were acting in concert.

Every protectionist measure has its downside, and this one has been no exception. EC chip prices have been maintained at an artificially high level causing EUROBIT (the European Association of Manufacturers of Business Machines and Information Technologies) to complain to the European Commission that DRAM prices were no longer competitive. On the other hand, the apparent certainty of pricing and margins has encouraged investment in fabrication facilities. Where once there was a single foreign semiconductor manufacturer in the EC, there were five (in 1990).

While the EC sees this type of protectionism as a needed time-out during which its industry can get up to speed and become competitive, the long-term effect will be debilitating. The quarterly revised fixed floor price negotiated under this agreement will cause customer anxiety over the financial and timing aspects of semiconductor purchases. In the long-term, the agreement is bound to encourage the kind of overcapacity and inefficiency that characterizes EC agricultural policy—inefficiency that leaves EC producers even less able to compete on local and world markets.

Europeans are not simply fighting for global market position from within. *In 1989, American electronics companies were acquired by European based firms in large numbers.* One-half of all such acquirers were British or French, while 10 percent were German or Swiss. The European acquisition strategy seems to focus on market position and vertical marketing—the same strategy American firms are adopting in Europe. American companies must take care not to overlook the effects of change in Europe on their domestic market.

The European Personal Computer and Software Industries

The European personal computer industry features a set of attractions which make it irresistible to domestic and foreign firms alike. The market is large and fragmented. New technologies and applications are developed every day. What's more, personal computer vendors can still depend on the inverse relationship between price and time.

An industry with so few barriers to entry was bound to be enveloped in policy warfare. Protectionist measures promulgated by the European Commission were to be expected, particularly in the face of the weakness of its home-grown industry. Unfortunately, where technology and production costs diverge, the objectives of sister industries may be in conflict.

Eleven American computer companies have formed the Computer Systems Policy Project (CSPP) for the purpose of advocating public policies which will boost the global competitiveness of American high technology industry. Specifically, CSPP is looking for long-term trade policies which will open foreign markets without necessitating state-managed trade. Unfortunately, this approach has put CSPP at odds with the American semiconductor industry. The computer firms have learned that they represent only part of America's hi-tech industry.

While U.S. chip makers complain bitterly of Asian products being illegally dumped on the American market, the computer makers have declared themselves pro-dumping under certain circumstances—circumstances that will guarantee that low-cost semiconductors remain available for American computer makers, irrespective of their place of origin or pricing policy. CSPP believes that if the U.S. chip making industry cannot satisfy domestic demand for quality, supply, availability, and performance, then no anti-dumping measures need apply to the low-price foreign suppliers.

It should come as no surprise that the Semiconductor Industry Association has asked what the CSPP would do if the shoe were on the other foot and very low cost personal computers were being dumped on the American market with no price protection.

With European personal computer markets growing rapidly, the competition is fierce and every penny of cost counts. Personal computer market growth in Europe in 1989 was nearly 32 percent. According to International Data Corporation (France), the three largest markets—Germany, France, and the U.K.—accounted for more than one-half of the five million business PCs sold in that year. According to a survey by UFB Locabail of Paris, 82 percent of small and medium sized French businesses (with fewer than 200 employees) expected to have a PC by the end of 1990. In 1987, fewer than 50 percent had a PC.

American vendors have been very successful in Europe and have captured 35 percent of the unit sales in France. Aggressive Apple and Compaq continue to pick up market share at the expense of the European vendors and IBM whose market share seems to drop each year (16 percent in 1989).

The United Kingdom has been going through something akin to the Spanish Civil War. Its personal computer wars have left it as a training ground on which the battles between American and Continental computer vendors are being played out to the detriment of domestic vendors. American manufacturers, IBM, Compaq, and Apple, dominate the market, while European companies fall further behind (Figure 21). Philips, Siemens, and Nixdorf, for example, have been forced into major cuts and thousands of layoffs. As a result, British vendors have been dropping like flies, failing to stir the kinds of nationalistic sentiments that often dictate the survival of Continental firms in their home markets. Even Apple has managed to overcome the conservative British nature, while simultaneously appealing to the die-hard individualism of the French. So, where is the opportunity? Falling barriers, enhanced telecommunications, deregulation of financial services, consolidation of administrative documentation—all of these changes are resulting in the dramatic growth of European information needs.

The American dominance of Europe's PC market comes in spite of a 4 percent external computer parts tariff and a proposal to apply the 45 percent domestic origin rule to printed circuit boards.

American firms also dominate the software side of European personal and business computing. On a worldwide basis, software revenues account for 35 percent of total computer industry revenue.[7] That figure is expected to jump to 50 percent by 1995. While the world software market has been growing at a 20 percent annual rate, the European packaged software market alone

FIGURE 21:   THE PC MARKET PLACE
EUROPEAN SALES OF AMERICAN PC MANUFACTURERS

A.

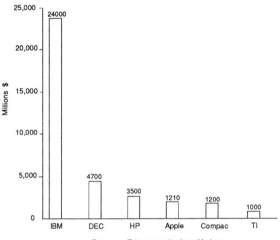

European Telecommunications Market

B.

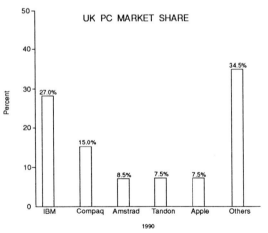

Total 1990 (est.) Volume: $2.75 Billion

Source: Rmark Research, National Association of Computer Dealers,
European Community

FIGURE 21:   THE PC MARKET PLACE
EUROPEAN SALES OF AMERICAN PC MANUFACTURERS
(Continued)

C.

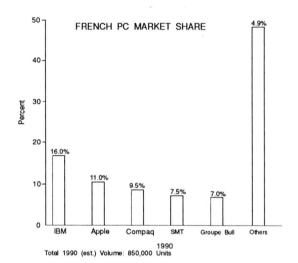

Source: Rmark Research, ADAPSO

represented over $16 billion, which will grow to well over $30 billion by the completion of the Single Market (Figure 22).

Software companies have more than just the competition on their minds when venturing into the EC. The software protection being granted by the EC is comparable to that of international literary copyright laws. Concern exists about just how strong that copyright protection ought to be. The issue has polarized the marketplace, leaving some large vendors (IBM, Digital Equipment, Microsoft, Lotus) at odds with less dominant companies (Groupe Bull, Ing. C. Olivetti & Co., Fujitsu, NCR, Unysis). These lesser competitors want interface specifications to be free of copyright protection. Such an arrangement would allow them to supply products for open system interchange (OSI) development and would maintain the health of the systems integration industry.

FIGURE 22:   EC RETAIL (PACKAGED) SOFTWARE MARKET

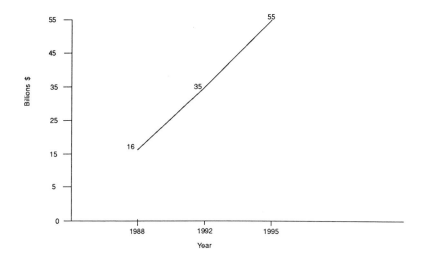

Source: Rmark Research, ADAPSO

The latter arrangement would allow products developed by dominant vendors to be open to a level of reverse engineering. The European Committee for Interoperable Systems (ECIS) lobbies in Brussels on behalf of the smaller players and has found support for less restrictive copyright protection.

The EC has taken a pro-protection stance, but is not likely to legislate Community-wide copyright protection any time soon. Listed among the five specific areas of "intellectual property" concern to the EC is the category of computer programs and databases. In late 1990, proposals for such protection were being drafted. The proposed computer software directive has been a controversial subject and is likely to include provision for selected reverse engineering where the objective is to allow interoperability rather than duplication (this is the version favored by the European Parliament).

For many American hardware and software vendors, Europe represents the opportunity to catch up after a late domestic start. Compaq and Apple have used innovation in terms of both product and marketing to capture large chunks of what was formerly IBM territory. The door is still open to Europe, particularly for creative vendors who can capitalize on large gaps left by the fallen European giants (Philips, Siemens) and on opportunities in some of the more marginal European economies.

The European Pharmaceutical Industry

The Single European Market is a mixed blessing for the pharmaceutical industry. On the one hand, a single pan-European drug testing and approval process would be a tremendous time and money saver for the introduction of every new European drug. According to the Cecchini (See Europeak appendix) report, *cost savings from mutually agreed upon drug registration procedures will amount to nearly 200 million ECU per year.* Three-quarters of that figure will come from in-process time savings. Without the mutual recognition and internal market reciprocity which will prevail in Europe, a new drug introduction could require at least twelve separate approval processes spanning several years and consuming millions of dollars of expense.

On the other hand, the relatively uniform availability of pharmaceuticals from country-to-country within the Community and elsewhere in Europe, means that the now disparate intra-country price structures are likely to give way to nearly uniform international pricing. Price competition will force international rationalization to which changes in shipping and global sourcing will contribute. In practical terms, this means that in those countries in which compounds were formally sold at a very high mark-up, drugs will now become competitively priced with those of neighboring states across whose borders products may now freely flow. While margins may shrink for such reasons, a mitigating factor may be the economies of scale that pan-European producers may now effect by rationalizing production and distribution.

The drug-pricing profiles of the EC countries are bound to change as a result. Germany, Denmark, and the Netherlands have traditionally been high priced countries, while Spain, Italy, Portugal and France have been the lower cost markets. The U.K. has typically occupied the mid-range.

As in most other product areas, the EC is anything but a uniform pharmaceutical market. *Each national group has a different historic national pattern of drug consumption and different medical traditions and practices.* Host country buying preferences (for health agencies) favor suppliers who maintain R&D or production in that country. National policies which have encouraged local drug formulation have resulted in significant inefficiencies, sometimes resulting in plants which operate at only 20 percent of capacity.

There are also different national price-setting and reimbursement regulations, each having a discriminatory effect. National health administrations maintain "positive" and "negative" lists of drugs, either limiting reimbursement to specific drug products only or excluding certain drugs or categories of drugs in their entirety. This kind of artificial limit on price competition often leaves pricing at the mercy of local scale production and neglects remote production, hurting overall efficiency. The effect of such an environment is a lower elasticity of demand for drugs than one might expect when income and pricing are varied.

It is clear, however, that the habits of Italian and French pharmaceutical companies will have to change. Both are too dependent on their local sales, sales that will now be threatened by companies invading their turf with comparable products at equivalent or better prices. U.S. and Swiss firms have already made their presence felt. This competitive effect is particularly true in the generic and over-the-counter drug field which already represents 50 percent of the market place.

According to Anna Persey of Prognos AG (Basel, Switzerland), *the EC pharmaceutical industry is highly concentrated and dominated by about sixty globally operating companies.* Thirty three of these companies are EC- based, twenty U.S.-based, four Swiss, and three Swedish. Until quite recently, pharmaceutical marketing has been conducted exclusively on a country-by-country basis, while R & D has been centralized in the country of origin.

The role of smaller companies varies considerably from country to country. More than 2,000 smaller companies do business in the generic and over-the- counter drug category. However, most of these companies participate only in their local markets. While they may have as much as 25 percent of the market in France or Germany, small companies have almost no market share in the U.K.. The minor, EC-wide impact of these smaller companies is testified to by the fact that 80 percent of the pharmaceuticals sold in the EC are produced by only 3 percent of the manufacturers.

The issue of protection of intellectual property is of major importance in the pharmaceutical industry. With product development and approval time horizons stretching to ten years and costs amounting to the tens of millions of dollars, companies can ill afford to let competing firms cannibalize sales by duplicating newly developed drugs. European patent protection was unified in 1978, mutual recognition of drug registration is now in place, and a series of intellectual property directives now affords Community-wide protection.

The lengthy new drug registration period has created a demand on the part of industry for extended patent protection. In the spring of 1990, the European Commission proposed a regulation that would extend the pharmaceutical patent term. The twenty year life of an EC drug patent may have a practical life of only five or six years under current testing and registration procedures. The supplementary protection certificate proposed by the Commission will allow member states to add another ten years to a drug's patent protection.

However, because the certificates will be issued by member states, twelve separate applications and approvals will be required for a single drug.

While some over-the-counter market niches may promise opportunity, the dominance of the drug market by large, multinationals limits new entry to specialized products which can capture unusually strong retail distribution.

The European Insurance Industry

The European Community accounts for 22 percent of the world insurance market—a $220 billion portion of a one trillion dollar market. While the U.S. and Japan account for 43 percent and 20 percent respectively of the world market, the EC is anything but small potatoes. The life insurance market alone in Europe is $90 billion. European Community-based insurers control nearly 60 percent of the worldwide reinsurance market.[8]

In 1984, non-European companies controlled nearly one-quarter of the EC insurance market, while only 10 percent of the U.S. market was controlled by non-U.S. insurers. Deregulation of the European financial markets is presenting unique opportunities for American insurers as well as those previously bound by intra-European restrictions.

In 1986, the European Court of Justice decided that small insurance policy holders should be entitled to more protection than large commercial clients until Community-wide harmonization was reached. Directives now define large risks as companies with over 250 employees, revenue of 12.8 million ECU, and balance sheet assets of 6.2 million ECU. Mass risks are small businesses and individuals. On a Community-wide basis, the ability to sell to individuals remains limited. A directive allowing cross border services for large risks was effective in mid-1990, and covers non-life risks.

Germany is Europe's largest insurance market—so large, in fact, that its private insurers dominate most

EC market segments. German dominance has spawned a variety of expansion strategies by large and small companies alike.

Five good sized European insurance companies have taken advantage of new EC corporate laws to form a EEIG (European Economic Interest Grouping). GMF (France), SMAP (Belgium), Societe Europeenne D'assurance (Luxembourg), HUK Cobourg (Germany), and Nueva Corporation (Spain) have formed the EEIG in order to take advantage of their common specialty. Each is actively soliciting and servicing public servants in its local market. With over seven million policies already in force, the group sees wide opportunity for expansion in newly available markets.

The consolidation that is normally expected in a suddenly deregulated marketplace also characterizes the EC insurance market. Groupe Assurance Generale of Belgium merged with AMEV of the Netherlands in 1990 in a transaction valued at $4.5 billion—all in an effort to better compete with the German industry giants.

Europe's biggest insurers, in terms of their worldwide premium incomes, are Allianz of Germany, U.A.P. of France, and Royal of the United Kingdom. The character of each of the home markets of these three giants has forced their conversion to global firms.

Allianz, for example, faces a highly regulated German market dominated by private insurers. Like its local competitors, it maintains a captive sales force. In fact, 70 percent of new *German insurance business is generated by captive agents or employed salesman. German insurance companies have strong personal relationships with clients, generally restricting the opportunity for brokerage services.* The EC estimates that 16 percent of the German population is over sixty-five years of age and that by the year 2030 that figure will be 28 percent.

On the other hand, U.A.P. is one of the many state-controlled firms which dominate the French market. Distribution methods vary, however, and include direct representation as well as distribution through a variety of institutional channels. French banks are commonly in the life insurance business, operating through insurance subsidiaries. Unlike the German system, there are over 1,700 French brokers who distribute product. While the internal regulation of the French market is not nearly so restrictive as that of Germany, the distribution process is comparable in the sense that most institutional or individual distributors represent the products of only one company.

The French insurance market is the world's fifth largest. According to the estimates of the European Commission, there will be more retired people in France than workers by the year 2000.

By contrast, the United Kingdom is more like the U.S. insurance market, with limited regulation, independent insurance brokers, and a variety of channels of distribution for the products of the private British insurers. The Netherlands has a comparably deregulated market, but with the largest per capita pension fund reserves in the world.

The open and highly competitive British market carries with it a certain advantage as deregulation spreads to other EC markets. *In life insurance, British insurers have as much as a 30 percent price advantage over their Continental competitors. This advantage extends to casualty insurance as well.*[9]

As a consequence of their experience in highly competitive, relatively free markets, insurers in the U.K. and the Netherlands should be better prepared to deal with the New Europe than many of the German and French companies who to this point have tightly controlled their local markets. Comparable opportunities should be available to American insurers.

The investment side of the insurance business in Europe is complicated by varying laws and requirements, which at some point in the distant future are to be harmonized. Insurance fund investors in Europe have been using the ECU rather than the dollar to denominate the equity and debt positions in their portfolios. There are even ECU-denominated offerings of life insurance policies and savings plans in the Netherlands, Luxembourg, France, and Italy. Corporate taxes have not been harmonized in the EC, so, for the moment, insurers can take advantage of differing tax rates by locating in the country with the most favorable tax policies (In Germany, the tax rate on retained earnings is 56 percent, while it is only 35 percent in Spain).

The effects of local tax policies on insurance and investment products continue to be anything but harmonized. There is a measure of tax relief in France, for example, if one invests up to 7,000 French Francs in a security. But in the U.K., a new product would want to take advantage of the rule that allows 4,800 pounds sterling to be invested in a "personal equity plan." Such differences are likely to bring continued success to domestically- generated instruments at the expense of pan-European funds.

Some of the important characteristics of other significant EC insurance markets are shown on the following page.

While the opportunities may be enticing, the key questions for outsiders seeking to enter or further develop in the EC insurance market are:

- What product and service advantages can we offer in the new market?

- Are local and EC-wide laws likely to restrict our efforts to market and service our products either locally or across the EC?

- What distribution alternatives are available both locally and throughout Europe?

- What cultural considerations need to be understood?

- How will existing competitors respond to our entry?

The European Environmental Industry

Americans see the Mediterranean coast as the stuff of vacation fantasies. Daily travel to and from a gray, Midwestern office in the dead of winter brings dreams of pristine, sandy beaches and crystal-clear water.

The member states of the European Community have 37,000 miles of Mediterranean and other beachfront, and yet, according to the European Commission, this unique natural resource is at risk due to inadequate sewage disposal in every member state—nearly all of whom are being sued or investigated by the Commission. In 1990, The United Nations Mediterranean Action Plan (Athens) estimated that *more than 20 percent*

GUIDE:	SECONDARY EC INSURANCE MARKETS

Country	Comment
Belgium	One-half of its 300 insurance firms are headquartered in other EC member states. Belgium encourages some investment of pension funds in non-traditional ways.
Italy	Insecurity of state-run pension funds is the spur to rapid growth in the private life insurance sector. Insurance is high cost. Deregulation has allowed distribution of products in retail stores and by mail order, including a 3.5 million name book club mailing list, for example.
Spain	A young country with 90 percent of the population between the ages of sixteen and sixty-five without individual life insurance protection. (*See:* What's Happening in Europe: a status report.)
Switzerland	Direct mail is used to promote insurance in this market more than any other in Europe. Sweden, Germany, and Belgium are also users.

of the EC's Mediterranean beaches were too polluted for swimming.[10]

With the bubble now burst, there is general recognition that Europe's environmental problems are every bit as serious as those of the United States, and in many cases, considerably more so. Acknowledged for some time to be as much as seven or eight years behind the U.S. in regulating environmental excess, Europe now is taking a tough stance toward both the creation and clean up of waste. In fact, if there is a trend to be projected from current EC legislation, it is that environmental directives will become increasingly more severe over the next decade.

Western European environmental worries have been heightened by growing fears about the unmanageable nature and scope of Eastern European environmental problems. An area of such universal concern presents a truly multinational opportunity for American suppliers of environmental equipment and services.

While bureaucrats in Brussels have taken an active role in environmental regulation, they have yet to establish a central bureaucracy comparable to the U.S. Environmental Protection Agency. Though its purpose will change with further review, the newly established European Environmental Agency was designed to be little more than a clearinghouse of information. Separate environmental investment funds and "superfunds" are likely to follow.

Western Europe has good reason to worry about its neighbors to the East. Pollution in Central Europe is an overwhelming problem. Visitors who last set foot on Eastern soil more than forty years ago are shocked by the industrial stagnation, smog, and destruction to water and wildlife. *Poland, for example, creates five times more solid waste and sulfur dioxide per unit of GNP than does Western Europe.* As Eastern lifestyles begin to conform more to those of the West, demand for scarce resources (fuel) will begin to grow dramatically as well.

The pent-up demand for automobiles and consumer electronics in the East is almost unimaginable.

With its fulfillment will come an increase in pollution and a further decrease in environmental quality.

For example, the dramatic growth in cellular phone service that has been discussed elsewhere, will cause drivers to spend more time in their automobiles, and more pollution will follow. The introduction of plentiful supplies of VCR's to the East will mean higher electrical consumption and the burning of more fossil fuels.

The European pollution control market is in the very early stages of a twenty year boom. The only restraining factor will be the ability of both private and public enterprises to pay—both for the environmental cleanup and for changes in wasteful industrial processes that add to the problem (Figure 23). Until recently, Western Europe had been dumping over one million tons of its waste in East Germany every year. Not only is this disposal outlet no longer available, but the West is now obligated to clean up its own mess.

The business opportunities are apparent but not without pitfalls. The European Commission origianlly provided a $620 million fund for the purpose of encouraging and supporting environmental protection projects in Eastern Europe—a tiny fraction of the funding that will be required to make even a small impact on the problem.

Eastern Europe represents only a piece of the greater Continental opportunity. A small German firm, Berzelius Environmental Services, went public in 1990 and saw its share price double at the opening. Degremont, a French water treatment firm, expects a doubling of the European market for sewage systems before the year 2000. It bases its projections on the knowledge that only 35 percent of sewage in Southern France is currently treated at all.

In early 1990, there were estimated to be about 6,500 European firms in the environmental protection business. But of this number, more than 4,000 had 1990 sales of less than $8 million.[11] The fragmentation of the market is such that at each sign of opportunity, a wave

FIGURE 23:   ENVIRONMENTAL CONTROL IN EUROPE

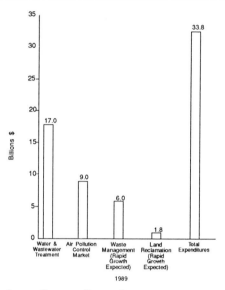

Source: European Community

of North American and Asian firms will join the flood of competitors seeking contracts. The sensitive political nature of clean up activities will dictate participation in consortia. Waste reduction equipment, systems, and services will require American technology, contributed through a series of partnerships with European vendors.

Waste Management Corporation, the world's largest environmental company, had difficulty breaking into the Western European market in the early '80s as it sought to acquire local waste management companies in Germany, France, and the Netherlands. Persistence paid off, as the company became better known on the Continent and built its European sales to over $700 million in 1989.

Finding strategically positioned European partners to whom U.S. companies can offer their technological and operating expertise continues to dictate success in a market that is lagging that of the U.S. in both its technological and regulatory aspects.

The European Consulting Industry

What do you get when you take Germanic, and French cultures, add Eastern spices and a touch of Latin flavoring and then mix vigorously? A European consulting boom. Under way since the late 1980s, this boom is following industry into a landscape littered with structural change.

With all of Europe thinking globally, large and medium-sized companies have begun to look within their ranks for managers who can handle fundamental change, develop organizations and strategies, deal with new geographic markets and opportunities, and take an aggressive stance toward expansion.

Many large organizations, unable to develop such managers internally, have engaged headhunters or personnel search consultants. These consultants are being assigned the task of finding managers with the broad experience and ability to deal with open borders, deregulation, and industrial restructuring. Not surprisingly, many of the executives that European search firms are discovering are coming from U.S. firms—firms that have been operating on a multinational, deregulated basis for a number of years. The United States, through its Procter and Gambles and Colgates, is inadvertently training Europe's current crop of Single Market managers.

Benefitting from this pan-European management restructuring are a handful of large search firms and a number of smaller industry specialists. Europe's largest search firms, in an industry growing at as much as 20 percent per year in billings, are Egon Zehnder International, Spencer Stuart, Russell Reynolds, Korn/Ferry, and Heidrick and Struggles.

The search consultants have had to adapt their own management styles to the structural changes in European industry. Heidrick and Struggles has ten European offices, organized geographically. One step above this "country management" in the company's corporate structure is a group of five practice leaders, each responsible for a particular industry group. The practice leader for financial services, for example, has pan-European authority and responsibility for searches that cross country borders.

Smaller American recruiters have been able to participate in the European boom through partnerships. Paul R. Ray and Company opened a London office but quickly learned that local credibility was required. In short order, it entered a partnership with the French firm, Carre, Orban, & Partners. Each firm now has access to the other's client lists and personnel databases. While the firms retain their identities, they acquire the international assets of the other.

In comparison to the U.S., European MBA's are relatively few and far between. As a consequence, companies compete fiercely for their services. If an MBA is not being recruited by a search firm for an industrial client, he may well be the object of a bidding war among corporate strategy consultants. Consultants are always on the prowl for associates with advanced degrees and language capabilities to fill multinational assignments.

Despite the talent shortage, the leading American strategy consultants have grown dramatically in Europe. From a standing start in 1979, Bain and Company has increased European billings to the point that they represent more than one-third of company revenues. In the past five years, Booz Allen & Hamilton has tripled its European revenue. Accounting firms, well received in France and the U.K., have aggressively pushed consulting services in fields ranging from information systems to less-than-truckload freight.

North American and European consultants stand to benefit in the extreme from cooperation in the early 1990s. As Europe undergoes almost daily change, American companies must be supplied with market research, competitive data, regulatory updates, and technical reviews. European consulting firms are clearly in a better position to supply that information than even America's largest, homegrown consultants—each of whom now has European headquarters and staff. Conversely, American consultants can give aggressive, global European companies the wherewithal to enter the U.S. market. Partnerships among American and European firms can give each access to clients in need of the expertise of the other.

As the consulting business itself becomes more global, smaller American consultants will be able to develop market niches based on transnational partnerships in a way that large American consultants have missed. The result of such partnerships will be the distribution of consulting "products"—industry research reports, multi-client studies, forecasts, and statistical surveys—to broad corporate constituencies in both Europe and North America.

The European Banking Industry

Eleven of the world's 100 largest banks (by assets) are based in the United States. However, America's largest, Citibank, is only ninth on the world list. Six Japanese and two French banks precede it in the top ten. Forty four of those top 100 banks are European-based banks. *What has happened to the grip that American banks once held on world finance?*

In 1980, the world's two largest banks were the U.S. flagships, Citicorp and Bank of America. Chase Manhattan was ranked thirteenth. But, according to the U.S. Federal Reserve Bank, the foreign assets of American banks fell from $343 billion in 1981 to $275 billion in 1988. In 1984, 163 U.S. banks had 917 foreign branches. By the end of 1988, 132 of the largest American banks had 849 foreign branches.[12]

Examples of American banks leaving European markets abound. Wells Fargo, the eleventh largest U.S. bank, once had twenty offices in Europe, South America, and Asia. It now has none. Chase Manhattan, among the world's leading bankers in the early 1980s is now thirty-second on the world list.

Both domestic and foreign regulation have conspired to relegate American banks to second tier lending status. As such, they have been forced to concentrate on niche market participation.

American banks have been progressively less able to compete on both a capital basis and in commercial loans. As a consequence, higher-margined activities have taken center stage. Securities trading and foreign exchange in London or Frankfurt, or investment advisory services, with the added advantage of having lower capital requirements, are now the primary focus. A more recent regulatory confirmation of the existing trend is contained in EC language concerning capital standards for banks. These include minimum capital adequacy rules and standards for weighing asset value against risk. The intent is that lower-risk assets will count further toward capital adequacy than equivalent amounts of higher-risk assets. *Many conservative Japanese and European banks, with Moody's highest AAA credit rating, are already ahead inthis game. Unfortunately, only two American banks have achieved equal status.*

Citibank is the only major American bank determined to forge ahead in Europe. It continues to enter as many markets and segments as possible and has over 700 offices in eleven European countries. Its strategy is at least partly dictated by its belief that future growth and success in its home market is inextricably linked to its success internationally.

Has the retreat from Europe and international banking in general adversely affected banking in the U.S.? Is this weakness a symptom of, or is it responsible for, the fact that foreign banks now control more than 25 percent of the business bank loans in the United States?

According to John F. McGillicuddy of Manufacturers Hanover Corporation, if good-sized, regional American banks choose not to stay or become international, "they will find not only that their growth factor is being restricted, but that they will have an increasingly

FIGURE 24:   THE DISMAL GLOBAL PERFORMANCE OF AMERICAN BANKS

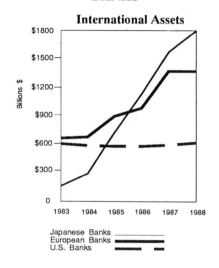

International Assets

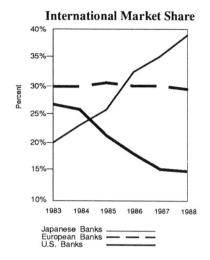

International Market Share

Sources: Federal Reserve System, Board of Governors Federal Reserve Bank of St. Louis

difficult job of maintaining the base of business they have at hand (in the U.S.)."[13]

Starting January 1, 1993, any EC subsidiary of a foreign bank will be able to operate anywhere in the EC by obtaining a single banking license from a member state banking authority. It is also likely that at the same time, a bank will be able to acquire a single investment license for brokerage, portfolio underwriting, or investment advisory services. The opportunity will exist for an American bank to perform a wider variety of business activities in Europe than it can domestically.

While the opportunity appears to be attractive, the competition already is building dramatically. Capital deficiencies and economic worries at home are likely to keep American banks out of aggressive expansion postures. However, from the point of view of the American industrial or service firm expanding to Europe, being forced into a relationship with a European-based bank will be a blessing. Such local relationships will effect the beginnings of the European profile that each new foreign competitor will want to foster. In addition, European bankers are generally closer to their European company clients than are American banks. Most European banks are also frequently stockholders in client companies. These same banks may be in a position to introduce potentially attractive joint relationships to their new American clients.

The European Cellular Communications Industry

The European Community is intent on modernizing and expanding its cellular telephone capabilities. No true pan-European cellular system is currently in place. In fact, Europeans entered the 1990s with a handful of incompatible analog systems in operation.

The Community has organized an effort to replace its technologically and physically limited systems with a single digital network having the capacity to manage many times the amount of traffic of its disparate analog predecessors.

The new EC cellular system standard, Groupe Special Mobile (GSM), was expected to begin extending coverage to seventeen European countries in mid-1991 and to replace the existing analog systems by year-end 1995. *The European Commission estimates that Groupe Special Mobile will create markets for equipment and services that will be worth more than twenty billion dollars by the year 2000.* An estimated one million lines in both analog and digital modes are expected to be installed by the turn of the century.

The Nordic Mobile Telephone System (NMTS), begun in 1982 and limited to the Scandinavian region, has been something of a barometer for European cellular demand and technological development. NMTS has a single operator and allows no reselling of air time—in contrast to the common North American practice. The problems of fixed phone line service associated with the severe Scandinavian weather have produced unusually high NMTS subscription rates. In Norway and Sweden, for example, forty of every 1,000 people have cellular service. This is in contrast to subscription rates of fourteen per 1,000 in the U.K. and less than three per 1,000 in Germany, France, Italy, and Spain.[14] *A single digital system across Continental Europe should foster an explosion in system usage.*

During the industry's early period of development, several different systems of regulation were put into place. The United Kingdom, with a subscriber base equal to one-third of that of all Europe (there were almost one million British cellular subscribers in early 1990), has permitted foreign companies to enter its markets as resellers, buying airtime from operators and reselling it to subscribers. Vodaphone and Cellnet are the system operators in Great Britain, and both are prohibited by law from selling air time.

While American-based Motorola, Bell South (Air Call Communications), and Millicom have penetrated the U.K. subscriber market (Motorola and Millicom each control more than 10 percent of the market), Vodaphone has invited Ericsson (AXE switches) and Matra SA of France (base station controllers) to provide equipment. Cellnet is being supplied by Motorola—already a supplier of networks to Austria as well as to one-half of the U.K. market.

Every one of the major European players is getting a shot at GSM contracts. Even national preference cannot seem to overcome the importance or price of state-of-the-art technology. While Ericsson, Siemens, and Nokia Oy compete fiercely on an individual basis for new contracts, each has joined its competitors to form consortia in order to increase the probabilities of landing one or more GSM contracts. One such consortium includes the French equipment suppliers Alcatel and Matra along with Germany's AEG, Finland's Nokia, Sweden's Ericsson, and the U.K.'s Orbitel.

American companies are seen as attractive consortium partners as well. U.S. companies can trade their technical expertise for access to European political connections and distribution. Europe affords North American companies an opportunity to acquire subscribers at a relatively low cost by selling air time. What's more, this entree may position the new competitor for participation in other lucrative markets and segments in the future. In one such instance, Motorola and some European firms are actively trying to interest the German and French governments in airtime reselling. At the same time, the German PTT is looking for a combination of direct selling and airtime reselling.

In well established markets, like the United Kingdom, luring subscribers, while lucrative, is costly and competitive. Promotional give-aways abound and often involve jewelry or airline incentives.

Other European players are seeking partners with attractive new technologies or political influence and saleable market expertise. A Mannesmann-led group, which includes Pacific Telesis, won a $6 million German cellular contract, at least partly because the German PTT was actively looking for foreign partners to teach it how to run a competitive network. The German PTT selected Trilogue's Infinity Message Management System to supply integrated voice and facsimile service on the German "C" cellular telephone network. While, the immediate German goal was to support 100,000 1990 subscribers, the network already had 200,000 subscribers by the end of 1989 and was growing at a rate of 6,000 per month.

Another American hi-tech firm, Comverse Technology, developed a new dialing plan for German cellular phones in conjunction with its German distributor, Ascom Gfeller AG. The new plan was designed to overcome a lack of signaling technology common to most German cellular phones.

Ericsson has a joint venture with General Electric in cellular telephone handsets, a market expected to grow from several hundred thousand units a year in the late 1980s to over one million units in 1992. The installed base in the U.K. alone should grow from 1.1

million in 1990 to 1.7 million in 1993. Accordingly, the GSM phone market is expected to grow from a standing start to over 500,000 units by 1993. In 1990, Motorola had a 25 percent share of the U.K. handset market and supplied that demand from its 70,000 square foot mobile equipment plant in England.[15]

Few domestic or foreign markets will match the growth profile of the European cellular market for the foreseeable future. This is an opportunity of which both large and small American firms can take advantage based on technological innovation and expertise. New strategic alliances are taking shape every day in the form of consortia that focus on very specific niche markets. The very composition of such groups circumvents national origin requirements while leaving the American partner highly involved in the direction and profitability of the enterprise.

The European Electrical Connector Industry

The electrical connector market is of interest, not so much because of its dramatic growth, but because of its segmented growth. Overall, European connector growth promises to be little different from that of the U.S. connector market. Yet, within Europe, some markets are clearly more attractive than others.

According to Elsevier Advanced Technology Research (U.K.), the European electrical connector market amounted to $2.5 billion in 1988. Growth of 4 percent per year will bring the market to just under $3 billion in 1992. *The German market is expected to comprise about 40 percent of the entire European connector market in 1992.* The Italian market, while growing at a 5 percent rate, will still represent only 7.8 percent of the overall European market in 1992.

The European Automatic Test Equipment Market

The European push to become more competitive with the U.S. and Japan is based in part on improved industrial productivity. The automatic test equipment industry exists for that very reason and logically stands to benefit from the increased demand for industrial efficiency and automation. *ATE manufacturers are counting on common European technical standards to help make their own businesses more productive.* Common standards ought to allow a streamlining of product lines and allow for the sale of a single product model in many different countries.

One market segment in which American producers are likely to quickly pick up market share is that of in-circuit board testers. This $200 million European market is growing at an 8 percent rate and is one in which American manufacturers have overcapacity while their European counterparts have too little.

FIGURE 25:   EUROPEAN ELECTRICAL CONNECTOR MARKET

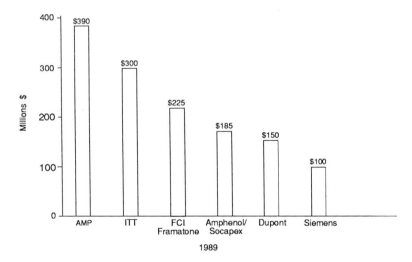

Sources: AEA, National Electronic Distriburors Assn., Elsevier Advanced Technology

High labor costs make the German market an attractive target for foreign ATE vendors. The West German ATE market was about $50 million in 1989, and has been dominated by strong local companies. Rohde & Schwarz GmbH, the market leader, does more than 30 percent of its business in Germany alone, fighting off the likes of Hewlett Packard, the leading American supplier. But H-P has had unusual success in this market due to its long-standing presence and positioning there as a "local" German company.

Perhaps the most rapid application growth for ATE over the next few years will be in the telecommunications field. With the opening of public procurement, vendors like GenRad are diversifying away from dependence on the national PTT's and are positioning themselves as global telecommunications suppliers. Service in the form of customization and development is becoming increasingly important.

Spea, an Italian board tester manufacturer, is using unusual customer service to grow at 20 percent per year. The $30 million company has gone from being the Italian market leader to the leader in its specialized segment throughout Europe. Thirty five percent of its sales now come from Germany, for example. In its efforts to win over customers to its unusual technology it will often leave its high-priced machine at the potential customer for as long as a year in order to win his business. Spea has forged an agreement with Testerion Laboratories in order to penetrate the American market as well.[16]

The European Fiberoptics Industry

The European market for fiberoptics was $875 million in 1987 and is growing at 15 percent a year. *Europe represents about one-half of the world fiberoptic market.* According to Prognos AG (Basel, Switzerland), the market should reach $2 billion by 1993.[17]

American vendors of fiberoptic equipment (cable, transceivers, connectors) have grabbed 35 percent of the market—a market dominated by telecommunications applications. Some of the national markets will outpace even this optimistic forecast. The Spanish market, for example, is expected to grow at an annual rate of 30 percent through 1993 and has been given a big push by the international communications links needed for the Barcelona Olympics. Fiberoptic applications within the European data communications markets are also achieving 30 percent annual growth.

The European Consumer Electronics Industry

Dutch giant, Philips, controlled the greatest share of the $20 billion Western European consumer electronics market in 1990. Its 28 percent market share was nearly double that of runner-up Thomson with 15 percent. Philips and Thomson were followed by the familiar Japanese competitors, Sony and Matsushita, each with 12 percent.[18]

A far-flung conglomerate, Philips has increasingly focused on its profitable consumer electronics business. In 1988, 32 percent of the company's profit came from consumer electronics on just 12.3 percent of its sales. The EC has worked to protect this market by imposing anti-dumping duties of up to 34 percent on Japanese CD players. To the benefit of non-EC vendors, however, is the EC decision to accept the GATT position against the "screwdriver assembly" rule.

Meanwhile, Philips has actively pursued the American CD and television market, at one point getting a single, $150 million order for TVs, video recorders, and satellite dishes from Whittle Communications. While the American weakness in consumer electronics has invited European and Japanese advances, Philips' advances have been tempered by internal troubles manifested in a company-wide retrenchment, personnel cuts, reorganization, and significant financial losses.

While they are aimed primarily at Far Eastern countries, the imposition of Community-wide quantitative restrictions will put a limiting effect on imports, particularly those American products that are assembled in Asia. *The EC bias against what we might call "Japanese" industries is so strong that American vendors would be wise to avoid market entry in any way other than the most subtle, i.e., as a supplier to or a minority partner of a key European player.* Legislative pressure on exporters of consumer electronics is likely to continue for many years to come.

The European Franchising Industry

France is the home of European franchising. *The Institut de Recherche et de Formation de la Franchise (IREFF) lists 1,800 franchisers and 100,000 franchisees in the European Community.*[19] Forty percent of these are located or based in France. Franchising is a growing enterprise elsewhere on the Continent as well, as deregulation of many markets stirs the entrepreneurial instinct in service-oriented Western Europeans.

Before German unification, it was estimated that franchising might account for 30 percent of all West German retail sales by 1992, and more than two-thirds of total sales volume in the services.

Franchising has taken root in the restaurant business and reflects the growing numbers of two-income families in both Northern and Southern Europe, as well as a growing number of pensioners in the North. The American trends toward convenient foods and services to an aging population are being replayed in Europe. Many of the strategies used in the American consumer service sector to capitalize on age-group markets will be effective in Europe as well.

The European Venture Capital Industry

The Single Market's commitment to the free movement of capital has made Europe more financially aware than it has ever needed to be. As money moves freely across borders, so do investment ideas and schemes. The leveraged buyout, already popular in the U.K., is making inroads on the Continent. The British equity markets give investors an exit vehicle that is considerably better developed than are those of most other European markets. *The growth of the venture capital industry closely tracks the increasing sophistication of the Continental securities markets.*

European investment markets have lower risk and taxation profiles than do those of the U.S. In order for American venture capitalists to take advantage of changes in both European market structure and attitudes, subsidiaries are being established that accept European venture capital as a local business. The new partners must be "real" Europeans, while the opportunity focus is on businesses that can be quickly taken to public equity markets or that are attractive acquisition candidates.

American venture capitalists have identified Spain and Switzerland as good sources of low technology deals, while Germany, France, and the U.K. are fertile markets for hi-tech deals, particularly in software-related fields. Success in European venture capital is likely to be concentrated in consumer product niches since the overall European Single Market sees its hope for the foreseeable future in the growth and success of its large national champions.

The European Advertising Industry

The European advertising market is only one-half the size of that of the U.S. This is largely due to the comparatively slow development of commercial television in Europe. But with the deregulation of the broadcasting market, advertising revenues will grow rapidly. *The overall advertising market in Europe is growing at 12 percent per year and promises to accelerate.*[20]

American advertising firms have already begun taking steps to position themselves in several of the key European markets. Grey Advertising, for example, spent $25 million in 1987 and 1988 buying a handful of advertising agencies in several EC markets.

Broadcast directives and the likelihood of considerably increased television viewing time over the next decade will dictate a broad increase in the effectiveness of broadcast advertising. American consumer product companies will want to develop relationships with strong, pan-European advertising firms in order to position themselves favorably in several geographic markets and to take advantage of media expansion.

The European Broadcasting Industry

American companies sold $700 million worth of television programming in Western Europe in 1988. *Reliance on foreign programming has compelled the EC to institute a broadcast directive which emphasizes the creation of local programming at the expense of imports.* According to the directive, more than 50 percent of the programming that is broadcast must originate in the EC wherever practical. At the same time, advertising can account for no more than 15 percent of the total daily transmission time and no more than 20 percent of any given hour. Commercial breaks will be allowed every twenty minutes, or forty-five minutes in the case of movies. These advertising limits apply only to cross-border broadcasts.

In issuing this directive, the European Commission had in mind to insure that local programmers be given the incentive to develop their trade, and ultimately compete on a global scale with the American programmers. Nevertheless, many Europeans think that the broadcast directive makes little sense. The critics believe that it is confrontationally protectionist, and that it is bound to bring a protectionist reaction, particularly in the wake of the often unpleasant GATT negotiations. Furthermore, many Europeans recognize that Europe is simply not sufficiently sophisticated in broadcasting to effectively use the breathing space given it by the directive to catch up to the leaders. It is more likely that the second-rate programming already available from local sources will simply be augmented, and that the growing sophistication of the industry will be retarded.

Critics also point out that there can never be a truly single European broadcast market because of permanent national language and cultural barriers. Single-Europe strategies on the order of Rupert Murdoch's newspaper, The European, are bound to fail. Only on a business level is English sufficiently universal to appeal to a wide European audience.

The European Leisure & Entertainment Industry

The United States has effectively exported its entertainment industry to Europe in the form of movies and television programming and is becoming increasingly effective at duplicating this success in both the sports and leisure markets. International television broadcasting of sporting events has created a global demand that has seen American-style football and baseball leagues spring up all over the Continent. This exposure is followed by a growing demand for the equipment that is necessary to compete in these sports.

While golf began in Europe, American equipment manufacturers and course designers have long dominated the industry. Meanwhile, a golf boom has overtaken Europe. According to Sports Illustrated,[21] the number of golfers in Europe has grown 240 percent since 1975. There are now 2.5 million golfers in Europe, and annual growth of more than 20 percent is being experienced in Finland, Austria, Sweden, Belgium, and Norway. Even in Norway, which had only twelve courses in 1990, twenty-eight more were under construction. Sweden, with 207 courses, had 101 under construction. France had 253 additional courses under construction in mid-1990. The U.K., with 2,300 of Europe's 3,500 golf courses, was asked by the Royal and Ancient Golf Club of St. Andrews to build 691 more by the year 2000.

Perhaps the greatest opportunity for golf equipment manufacturers in Europe will come about through the aging of Northern Europe's population. In the United States, golfers who are over fifty years of age make up 25 percent of the golfing public but play 51 percent of the rounds—three rounds for every one played by a twenty-five-year-old.

The "graying" of Northern Europe will influence more than just the demand for golfing equipment. Manufacturers of fishing and camping equipment as well as those of leisure shoes and clothing are already seeing business growth.

Elsewhere in the entertainment and leisure field, the market awaits legal action. In video and audio recording, the market is being damaged by the sale of illegally copied recordings amounting to as much as $20 million annually in each member state.[22] A Community-wide copyright law, while it would be a great boon to the producers of this and other like material, is not likely soon. Instead, the European Commission is trying to establish a series of penalties for violations in five areas: piracy, sound and audio-visual home copying, distribution and rental rights, computer programs and databases.

The confluence of rapidly "Americanizing" European consumer tastes and the aging of Northern Europe's populace will present a series of opportunities for products and services that cater to these changing tastes and demographics.

The European Defense Industry

The sudden end of the Cold War has caused the European defense industry to closely examine its core businesses. Many European conglomerates with defense-related subsidiaries or divisions have subsequently chosen to divest themselves of these operations for fear that the future promised little growth and ever increasing bureaucratic complications.

While most cash-short governments jumped at the chance to downscale defense spending, some again took up the banner of increased spending in order to bolster the local economy. Former French Defense Minister Jean-Pierre Chevenement said on Bastille Day, 1990, that due to his expectation of economic and military instability in Europe, France would build up its military and maintain an independent nuclear capability. While subsequent events may have vindicated his stand, it should not be overlooked that France is the world's third largest weapons exporter and gains economically from any such political or economic uncertainty.

While the European defense industry was hit hard by the relaxing of East-West tensions in the late 80s, the Euro Fighter Aircraft (EFA) remained a much sought after and publicized project.[23] A joint project of the U.K., Germany, Italy, and Spain, the EFA represented to many the future of the European defense industry. For this reason, European technology was chosen where ever possible, even when it may have been incompatible with commonly used American-built aircraft. Ferranti Plc. (England) was banking on the EFA contract to help bail it out of financial difficulty. Competing for a $3.2 billion contract with a consortium consisting of Daimler-Benz and GEC-Marconi, Ferranti pitted its radar technology against a Hughes Aircraft system being proposed by the consortium.

Desperate for a prop for its own defense business, GEC-Marconi persuaded the British government to go along with its acquisition of Ferranti Defense Systems

Group. It was then announced that the Ferranti radar technology would be used in the EFA contract bid. Consolidation of the industry was imperative to insure any home-grown survivors at all, and the guarantee of local technology was a sufficiently significant bargaining chip to assure the approval of an otherwise monopolistic merger.

Securities analysts have predicted that defense spending in Europe will fall 7 percent between 1990 and 1993. This has prompted a slew of mergers and acquisitions. According to Hoare Gorvett, (U.K.), 16 European defense companies with revenues of $8.4 billion were sold in 1989—-90. In addition to the GEC-Ferranti combination, Daimler-Benz bought Messerschmidt ($4 billion); Thomson-CFS signed a joint venture agreement with British Aerospace ($1.2 billion); Thomson bought the military businesses of Philips in Holland, Germany and France ($700 million); and, Siemens acquired Plessey's European radar and communications group ($420 million).

Philips rid itself of defense assets in order to better focus on telecommunications and non-military electronics. The acquisition of these units by Thomson-CFS solidified Thomson as Europe's leading defense conglomerate.

Even with isolated pockets of activity, the defense business as a whole will be unable to support all of the existing competitors. The future is best seen in the actions of a large service organization with locations throughout the Continent. With its primary business being the service of equipment and vehicles at allied military bases, company management quickly reacted to the "demilitarization" trend in Europe. A pan-European strategic consulting firm was hired to develop strategic business alternatives for the company. New, non-military applications of its service expertise and network were found and a strategic approach was formulated to enter these new markets. The future was clearly not to be in defense, but in unrelated fields to which its skilled workers could quickly adapt.

III

STRATEGIC ALLIANCES AND THEIR APPLICATION

8

The Strategic Alliance: The Key to European Market Penetration

Finding the Right Partner

In many ways, Europe has looked Westward, to America, with economic envy for over a century. The United States is often seen as a pattern against which Europe can compare itself and improve upon its unique economic and social character.

Americans take pride in capitalistic freedoms. The success of the economic system combines with the nation's plentiful natural resources to characterize the American psyche. The purchase by foreign buyers of American assets is more an injury to national pride than a competitive disadvantage in the global market place. For two hundred years the vitality of American growth was such that its pace overwhelmed that of the invaders. Those foreigners who came often never left—seduced by the American economic and social experience. The flame of that burning economic vitality was fanned by waves of immigrants from foreign shores, who, out of sheer desperation and hard work, forced entrepreneurial verve and business innovation down America's collective throat.

The prototypical spur to this economic vitality was the Eastern European immigrant—a refugee from a continent scarred by revolution, persecution, and violent institutional change.

*   *   *   *

My grandfather was such a man, coming to the United States from his native Europe at the turn of the century without money or friends. His name was Trachman. As he stood in the makeshift immigration center on Ellis Island— he listened intently to the conversations of those just ahead of him in line .

The first candidate for admission, managed to get the point across to the admitting officer that his vocational skill was carpentry. Without hesitation, the officer filled in the admissions identification form with the name "Carpenter" and ushered him off toward the next station in line. The next candidate, had so thick and guttural a German speech pattern that the admitting officer could make out nothing he said. Finally, after much gesticulating and grunting with frustration, the officer realized that the sweeping arm motions, delicate hand movements, and careful fingering of his garments was an indication of this would-be immigrant's skill with a needle and thread. Taylor became his name from that moment.

As my grandfather and these two equally lost newcomers stood outside the immigration center on Ellis Island, they took comfort from one another. And they made a pact. Every ten years, they would meet and exchange progress reports on their status in this great country.

Ten years passed and my grandfather graduated from the sweatshops of New York's Lower East Side to a business of his own—a grocery stand. He traveled from his home in Greenwich Village to the agreed upon meeting place by foot. His compatriots met him there as planned—

Carpenter, in fine clothes, arrived by cab. Taylor came by foot, but from some miles away, and his fatigue showed. The three men spent several hours together during which time it became clear that Taylor was the worst-off of the three. They parted that evening, Carpenter and my grandfather sharing a cab, and Taylor returning home the way he had come.

Ten more years came and went. My grandfather moved, to Newark, New Jersey, where he had both a stand at the farmers' market, and a sizable wholesale grocery business along side of those who would become the Pathmark and ShopeRite retail grocery chains. Carpenter now lived in Connecticut where he had become a real estate developer of some prominence.

When the time for their meeting came, my grandfather arrived first in his Chevrolet. Carpenter arrived in a chauffeur-driven Cadillac. Poor Taylor again arrived on foot. Unlike those of his friends, Taylor's clothes were well-worn to say the least. Neither my grandfather nor Carpenter could restrain himself. For hours they lectured Taylor on the methods that they had used to push themselves ahead in business, on salesmanship, and on their willingness to learn. Taylor was overwhelmed by what he was hearing. Both of his friends had urged him to draw a partner into his business—preferably one with some capital or clout.

As Taylor left this meeting, he wandered despondently past a small house of worship on Manhattan's Lower East Side. Evening had already fallen, and, as he opened the door and entered, he found a group of men absorbed in prayer. He moved quietly to eastern wall of the room, closed his eyes, and began quietly and earnestly appealing to the Lord to help make him the success in business that his friends, Trachman and Carpenter, had become.

After some time, he left, a calmer, more contented man than the one who had entered a short time before, knowing that somewhere he would find the influential partner that he sought, and that this would, in turn, lead to his business success.

Ten more years passed. Trachman and his family had now moved from Newark to a large Spanish-style home at the Jersey Shore. Carpenter now lived in Greenwich, Connecticut, on a spacious estate. Trachman and Carpenter had kept in touch, but neither knew much of Taylor or what had become of him since their last meeting. Then, one day, each received a phone call from a woman, purportedly Taylor's secretary, asking that a rendezvous be arranged for the very next day outside a well-known mid-town Manhattan department store. Their curiosities piqued, each agreed immediately.

The following day, Carpenter arrived in his chauffeur-driven limousine, and my grandfather in his Cadillac. They waited for some time, but eventually their patience ran thin. As they prepared to leave, Carpenter noticed a chauffeur-driven Rolls Royce approaching. When the handsome sedan pulled to the curb, to their amazement, out stepped Taylor, attended by his secretary and executive assistant. Recovering from their shock, Carpenter and Trachman peppered Taylor with questions: When? How? Taylor paused and then launched into a recounting of the previous ten years. He reminded his friends of their suggestion that he take in a partner with "influence" and described his subsequent preoccupation with the idea. He then turned slowly toward the building in front of which they had been standing, identified it as his own, thanked them for their advice and pointed to the sign over the main entrance: Lord & Taylor!

*   *   *   *

Will we learn our lesson in Europe? Success there will depend on a number of factors, not the least of which will be staying power. But for those without the deep pockets necessary to ride out cultural or institutional resistance, the careful execution of partnership strategies will be essential. A joint venture or alliance is only as good as your ally. Will you choose wisely? Have you done your homework and the careful and extensive analysis of both the market and joint venture candidates that is required? Mr. Taylor, in the anecdote above, spent ten years preparing for and concluding his partnership search. Will you be able to do as well? What should you look for? How should you proceed?

9

The European Community and the Nature of Strategic Alliances

The partnership forged by the twelve members of the European Community is not very different from those being formed in the business world every day. Just as no single *company* can be all things to all customers, no single European *country* can provide the marketplace or resources required to accommodate the global desires of its multinational companies and consumers.

Strategic business partnerships, whether formed by acquisition or joint venture, are the springboards for renewed corporate growth. In a comparable way, each EC member state is investing in a partnership that can broaden its reach and renew its growth as both a trading partner and innovator in its internal market.

131

Why Strategic Alliances Make Sense

Strategic alliances have been used effectively by enterprises seeking to capture new products, methodologies, markets, and the spirit of entrepreneurial innovation. While a partnership position may or may not prove to be profitable in monetary terms, it is a firm commitment to a long-term growth strategy. No better way has been found to gain a foothold in an otherwise little-known market.

Scrutiny of the bottom line in such joint relationships can be tragically misleading. An income statement reveals very little about the progress made toward stated objectives. *The true measures of success are the development of the working relationship with one's partner and a steady movement up the learning curve.*

The "Joint-Venture is No-Venture" Mentality

In 1987, a major European capital equipment company developed what it believed to be a superior thermal destruction technology for the elimination of certain industrial hazardous waste products. Company marketing and engineering staff recognized that hazardous solids, liquids, and gases were being created at an alarming rate throughout the industrialized world. What's more, regulations affecting the disposal of these waste products were about to eliminate the most popular storage and disposal options. Even incineration, in some nations and regions, would soon become a less practical alternative.

The extension of the company product line to this new market seemed both a logical and advisable move. A trusted consulting firm was hired both to analyze the markets for the new thermal technology and to recommend the advisability and logistics of proceeding with its development and marketing.

Much to the surprise and chagrin of the client, the consultant was able to demonstrate convincingly that a meaningful market for such equipment did not yet exist. In addition, competition among incineration equipment suppliers and waste disposal services was fierce. The consultant also noted that the materials to which the new technique could best be applied, though growing in volume, accounted for only a small portion of the current waste market. Given the potential of technology technology in as little as five years, however, it was recommended that a partner with relevant market access and technical understanding be sought.

In retrospect, it is clear that this company was staring at a long-term opportunity to learn about and profit from markets to which its manufacturing and technical strength could be applied. Perhaps a low-risk, joint "nursing" strategy could have uniquely positioned its new product and expertise on the ground floor of an expanding market place. Yet, the decision of the company was to abandon its product development and its interest in the hazardous waste market place in its entirety. The Managing Director of the organization simply concluded, "A joint-venture is no venture."

What reasons could this executive have had to justify such nearsightedness? Perhaps he had been a party to one or more failed joint-ventures in the past. Did he categorize as failures all joint ventures which were ultimately terminated—measuring them only by their financial performance? Lost in such reasoning is the possibility that *his partnership may ultimately have changed the rules of the game by, in effect, advancing the starting line of the race in which his company had hoped to compete.*

The EC: A Joint-Venture Designed to Level the Global Playing Field

The twelve member nations of the European Community are partners in a joint venture with long-term ramifications. Europe wants to move the starting line in its race against North America and Asia—to reverse its lagging competitive fortunes. Each partner knows that for the short-term the effort may yield little in the way of profit. Independence will be sacrificed to a new, central bureaucratic structure in Brussels. Control of economic policy will be lost as tax rates and currencies are harmonized. National social structures may be altered by a social "contract" imposed by fellow EC members.

Fear, Loathing, and Brotherhood

One doesn't have to love the French to work with them. One needn't envy Germany's work ethic to understand its consumer and technological markets. It is just not necessary to be an afficionado of Spanish art to appreciate what the Spanish labor market and demographics can mean to a labor-intensive consumer business.

The EC is an uneasy agglomeration of disparate cultures and people, each of whom has an interest in long-term survival and prosperity. If that goal means short-term sacrifice, then so be it—at least for the moment. Fear and a common goal have carried the day. As is the case in corporate partnerships, EC members understand that *carefully constructed and fully enforceable agreements can make even seemingly intolerable marriages survive.*

Lest one think that the engagement of these twelve European cultures is endangered by puerile squabbling, reassurance can be found in periodic outbreaks of tactlessness and offensive rhetoric that have already been overcome.

Cooperation can often survive covert squabbling. However, when those disagreements become public knowledge, the dissolution of a partnership often follows. To Europe's credit—or perhaps more accurately, to the credit of its universal recognition that economic union must be achieved—the July, 1990, Nicholas Ridley affair has been acknowledged and dismissed. The realities of the New Europe have simply overwhelmed social, political, and economic prejudices.

Nevertheless, the Ridley affair is a significant reminder of the underlying biases which intrude on Continental unity and seek to undermine the alliance on both the macro and micro levels.

A minister in the British government and a close ally of then Prime Minister Margaret Thatcher, Mr. Ridley was frank, personal, and offensive in an interview with *The Spectator* in July, 1990. Clearly overcome by the breathtaking pace of change in Europe, and with the Second World War still fresh in his mind, Ridley accused the West Germans of trying to take over Europe: "You might just as well give it to Adolf Hitler, frankly," he said in the magazine interview. He betrayed no great love for his French neighbors either, accusing the French government of "behaving like poodles to the Germans." Attacking the European Monetary Union, steadfastly stonewalled by the British at the time, he described the EMU as "all a German racket designed to take over the whole of Europe. It has to be thwarted." "There could be a bloody revolution" if monetary union succeeds. The power of the German mark would dominate any Continental monetary system, he stated. According to Ridley, "Being bossed by a German, it would cause absolute mayhem in this country, and rightly, I think." "I'm not sure I wouldn't rather have the (bomb) shelters and the chance to fight back, than simply being taken over by economics." "(The German people) are already running most of the Community."

Although Ridley resigned within a few days of the interview's publication, it was clear that he had the sympathy of the Prime Minister. The magazine interviewer summed up the feelings of many Britons, saying, "why should someone resign from the British government because he has offended the Germans?"

Shortly thereafter, a memo was published describing an earlier Thatcher meeting with several British scholars on the subject of Germany. The group, which also included the British Foreign Secretary, described Germans in terms of "their insensitivity to the feelings of others, their obsession with themselves, a strong inclination to self-pity, and a longing to be liked." Less flattering features used to describe typical Germans were "angst, aggressiveness, assertiveness, bullying, egotism, inferiority complex, sentimentality, a capacity for excess, (and) a tendency to overestimate their own strengths and capabilities." As if to justify this exercise in analysis, the memo records the conclusion that "we should be nice to the Germans" because they are now more prepared to confront their shortcomings.

Despite its lack of trust in both Germany, and an unelected EC bureaucracy, Britain and Mrs. Thatcher announced agreement to join the European Monetary System only three months after the Ridley affair. Her late 1990 protests not withstanding, it seems inevitable that economic union, and perhaps even political union will be acheived, beginning in the mid-1990s. The risk of EC failure and the union's potential long-term benefit are simply too great to justify the continued assertion of British independence.

Knowing What You Are Up Against

A 1990 Korn/Ferry International polling of the chief executives of major American corporations found that 68 percent of those responding to the survey agreed that global competition would be the greatest challenge for business in the next century. On the other hand, *fewer than 20 percent of those same respondents believed that foreign language capability was very important*. In similar surveys of Europeans, Japanese, and Latin Americans, 75 percent of those polled believed language facility to be of extreme importance. The survey also found that most American executives believed overseas experience to be less important than did foreign executives.

If Americans are to effectively penetrate the rapidly coalescing "fortress Europe," they will do so selectively, but with a sensitivity to the cultures and nuances of doing business away from home. Americans trained in infinitely large and growing domestic markets may be rudely awakened by a segmented and protective market place that is not at all the Common Market that the United States once envisioned.

Great Expectations

When the post-war American investment in Europe succeeded in rebuilding the Continent's tattered economies, the Common Market became a dream with merit on both sides of the Atlantic. Both the U.S. public and private sectors were enamored of the concept of a single continental market for three primary reasons.

First, beginning in the Eisenhower administration, Americans began to look actively for a way out from under at least part of the burden of European defense. An economic and political union among the Western European nations promised to provide an incentive to build an effective European defense under a mutually dependent umbrella.

In addition, a European union had the ability to encircle and lock Germany within it. Today, with a reunified Germany, the concern is doubly significant, as expressed, however tactlessly, in the remarks of Mr. Ridley.

Finally, the American concept of European union has always been dependent upon the leadership of Britain. The market-based British economy promised the kind of free trade that Americans wishfully envisioned for all of Europe. In fact, Britain's economy is more closely tied to the U.S. today than to the Continent with nearly 60 percent of British foreign investment in the

United States, three times that invested on the Continent. In short, the expectation was that Europe would become an extension of our own fifty-state single market.

While Europe has attained a measure of each of these expectations, reality has fallen far short of desire. American investment in European defense was unaffected by the growing European union. It, in fact, grew from conventional to nuclear proportions. The reunification of Germany has created a newly threatening psychology for all of its neighbors as well as for countries for whom the memory of two wars and a Holocaust do not quickly fade. Less desirable still is the ascension of the New Germany to a position of financial leadership in the EC. It's currency and economy dominate those of the other member states. The combination of Germany and its largest trading partner, France, and their protectionist/socialist ways has been too much for free trade advocate, the U.K., to overcome. In place of the open EC envisioned by early American supporters, has come a selectively protectionist set of local markets, governed by a new central bureaucracy.

Where Do We Go From Here?

The European Community is not, and will never be, the United States of Europe. The federal system employed in America is quite different from the evolving European system. The American system, for example, clearly differentiates between the powers of the state and those of the federal government. The EC, by contrast, has no clear separation of powers between Brussels and the member state governments. While taxes, social policy, and environmental safety are political considerations for the EC, they are commercial market matters for the U.S. For reasons of economic survival, tax harmonization in the United States of America makes no sense at all, yet in Europe it is a key to expanding and unifying a fragmented economic market place.

References to a "European Superstate" have punctuated British thought since Brussels began asserting itself in the mid-1980s. Jacques Delors said in 1988 that in ten years, 80 percent of Europe's economic legislation would be generated by the law makers in Brussels rather than by those in the member country capitals. The very bureaucratic, central authority and control that Mrs. Thatcher had fought so hard to eradicate in the U.K. is being reimposed by the EC from Brussels. But, of course, her objections are valid in so far as they affect the independence and economic approach of the U.K. The monetary union so cherished by M. Delors is the embodiment of that central control. A fixed common currency with exchange controls (to prevent money from seeking the best return across borders) also means restricting the use of devaluations for political, social and economic reasons. The wage, work week, and other requirements of a social charter are equally restrictive and would eliminate many of the advantages of the more depressed EC regions, like Spain, Portugal, or Greece.

This is the genesis of the EC. It springs from the minds of socialists, who have adopted the free market moniker as a replacement for discredited economic theory. This reflects the political and economic right turn by Europe which occurred in the early 1980s with the elections of Thatcher and Kohl. Even doctrinaire socialists like Mitterrand and Gonzalez (Spain) were compelled to decontrol selected markets in order to appease the populace. Brussels is, after all, peopled by unelected officials, appointed by others who preside over populations with little experience of actually electing their governments. While the British electoral system has been in place for some time, the French have elected their governments only since 1958, and many of its neighbors only since the end of the Second World War.

With philosophies that now look surprisingly capitalistic, and liberal doses of free market language, Europe is a thinly disguised cartel—a cartel that is building *of the swing away from the birth and growth of new, innovative, smaller enterprises, and toward large inte-*

grated companies seeking control of large markets. The French overtly encourage this behavior on the part of their large companies. European bureaucrats are convinced that only this reinforcement of the large, national champions will protect Europe from Japanese and American domination. The entrepreneurial spirit is neither cultivated nor understood.

Protection of Europe's cartels has fostered the propogation of rules of origin — rules that have been imposed to buy time for the rebuilding of Europe's cartels and national champions. One needn't look much beyond the massive restructurings at Philips and Siemens to find support for this assertion.

In many ways, the EC is a response to the fact that many of these national champions have never been sufficiently global. The list below demonstrates that, even with much smaller domestic markets than their American or Japanese counterparts, the home market is still paramount for the EC's largest companies.[1]

Ericsson and Sony, with comparatively small or saturated markets at home, have emphasized the international for years. Each has done so by focussing on a

**GUIDE: FOREIGN REVENUES HAVE LAGGED AT MANY OF
EUROPE'S LEADING COMPANIES**

Company	% of Revenue from Foreign sources
Xerox (USA)	84%
Sony (Japan)	70%
Philips (Netherlands)(before restructure)	93%
Ericssson (Sweden)	78%
Siemens (Germany)	50%
Olivetti (Italy)	65%
Thomson (France)	60%
British Aerospace	66%
Racal (U.K.)	60%

relatively few products or industries. Ericsson, in particular, has taken a very pointed approach to EC participation. Contrast this with the broad internationalization of Siemens or Philips, each with hundreds of business units, many with no underlying relationship to the others (Figure 26).

FIGURE 26:   PROSPECTS FOR EUROPEAN INDUSTRY

Sectors	Annual Average Growth Rate in Volume for the Production of the Triad 1987-1993 (%)	European Share:
Software	15.0	
Semi-Conductors	12.3	
Data Processing Equipment	9.0	
Telecommunications Equipment	5.3	
Aircraft Construction	4.6	
Pharmaceuticals	3.7	
Telecommunication Services	3.7	
Consumer Electronics	2.8	
Machine Tools	2.6	
Electricity	2.3	
Food Industry	1.6	
Textiles, Clothing	1.0	
Automotive (Number of Cars)	0.6	
Raw Steel (Millions of Tons)	-1.2	

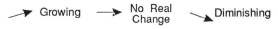

Growing   No Real Change   Diminishing

Source: BIPE-IFO-Prometeia, Swiss Bank Corporation

Real Growth, New Markets

With the saturation of many American markets and increased competition in others, the Single European Market presents potentially attractive opportunities for thousands of American goods and services. The economy of the European Community is expected to grow at an average annual rate of 3.5 percent throughout the 1990s, twice that of the 1980s. Much of that improvement comes as a result of a rush by Continental companies and governments to capitalize on the new market opportunities brought about by open borders.

For example, a 1989 opinion survey by the French magazine, *L'expansion*, demonstrated that a majority of French chief executive officers were planning to increase capital investment that year.

The $4.3 trillion EC economy is creating 1.5 million jobs per year, the greatest numbers in twenty-five years. The British unemployment rate fell from 12 percent to 7 percent in just three years. While 1990 Western European unemployment was nearly 10 percent, it had been falling and was likely to continue to do so on average, throughout the decade. Overall Western European inflation had fallen to 3 percent, its lowest level in twenty years, as a result of structural changes in fiscal and monetary policy. In 1988, wages across the Community rose only 3.8 percent, one-half of the rate of 1984.

The entire European infrastructure is being overhauled as well. The French government is spending $909 million to upgrade the highway system in Northern France. It has budgeted $3.3 billion for expansion of its high- speed train system. Both local and national authorities are working hard to reduce the bureaucracy involved in the economic development grant making process. In 1985 there were over 400 separate procedures to be executed by foreign firms seeking French national and regional grants and loans. By 1989 the number had been reduced to 200, only twenty of which were required 80 percent of the time. The French agency, DATAR, can now finance up to 25 percent of an investment that will create at least twenty jobs in three years for a company with worldwide sales of about $50 million when a $3.5 million minimum investment is being considered. DATAR grants can amount to $9,000 per job. As of 1990, 560 American companies employed 230,000 workers in France (Figure 27).

FIGURE 27:   GROWTH OF THE MAJOR WESTERN ECONOMIES

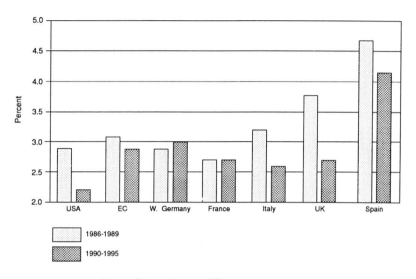

1986-1989
1990-1995

Source: Federal Reserve, EC

The Expanding Continent

Geographically, Europe is much more than just the European Community. While the EC has taken the lead, a variety of other alliances extend the New Europe beyond the twelve EC member states to include the Eastern European countries and the Mediterranean states as well. In addition to EFTA and the European Economic Space, other alliances have been formed, often based on historic connections. The Pentagonale—a trade, transportation, and environmental consortium of Italy, Yugoslavia, Hungary, Czechoslovakia, and Austria—is based on the old Hapsburg Empire. There has been discussion of a revived Hanseatic League, a fifteenth century alliance of 160 cities from London to Novgorod, now referred to as the Baltic Rim Alliance. This attempt to emulate the economic growth of the

Pacific Rim would include the Baltic states, the Russian Republic, Scandinavia, Germany, and Poland.

Outsiders Confront a Three-Fold Dilemma

As with all silver linings, a cloud exists. American and Asian firms confront a three-fold problem upon entering Europe's growing and unifying markets. First, they are presented with a new set of rules, dictated by a central authority in Brussels, which in some cases replaces national and regional regulations and in others simply adds an additional layer of anxiety. Greater resources than ever will be spent on legalistic and logistic considerations at the expense of the strategic.

Second, foreign firms, who often have been thinking internationally for many years, are now going to confront national and regional competitors who are thinking international for the first time. The level of competition has been raised as European firms grow, branch out, and acquire previously foreign technologies, staff, and philosophies. This is a strategic threat that won't go away and, in many industries, may effect domestic American markets as the emboldened European competitors invade the U.S. The serious work of internationalization was brought home to several large European "national champions" in a period of just a few months in early 1990, when a handful of chief executive officers of Europe's largest firms were fired, including those of Philips, Nixdorf, and Kuoni Travel. Global performance demands globally-oriented managers, starting at the top.

Finally, long-term fears of European protectionism are quite justified as are the threats of closed markets to outsiders in recessionary times. *The survival of a European presence in every significant market will be a policy that supersedes all free market considerations.*

When Politics and Economics Don't Mix

Those of us on the outside looking in need to be realists. Sure, the EC is a seductively available market in which to sell a variety of foreign goods. The strength and single-mindedness of the move toward unity is as impressive as it is attractive. But there will be rough roads ahead. The long-standing cultural and political animosities among many of the European nations, while overshadowed at the moment, are bound to surface with repeated economic downturns.

The EC's Common Agricultural Policy (CAP) has not pacified French farmers, for example. In the early autumn of 1990, they began intercepting, destroying, or diverting lower cost, imported meat from East Germany, the U.K., and Ireland. As a result, a movement was afoot in Britain to boycott all French products. A promise of EC-CAP relief of nearly $30 per unsold animal was still not sufficient to calm anxieties.

A single market is not likely to dictate a level playing field for member states who try to attract and keep investment either. Why are Fujitsu, Sharp, Intel, and others investing heavily in the U.K. and Ireland rather than in Germany? It has more than a little to do with the fact that German engineering salaries are often 70 percent higher than those in the U.K.

The excitement of a strong Spanish economic revival and its low-cost work force is a direct threat to the well established industrial economies of Germany, France, and the U.K. The invasion and subsidization of low-cost Eastern European goods will rally protectionist sentiment as well.

At a meeting of the World Business Forum in late June, 1990, former West German Chancellor, Helmut Schmidt, predicted "turmoil, bitterness, and high unemployment" in the Eastern European countries for some years to come. The Forum attendees agreed that rebuilding economies, environmental problems, and poverty could increase protectionist pressures throughout Europe.

Like so many alliances, internal pressures will cause cracks in the walls. As outsiders, American and Japanese firms need to insinuate themselves into the fabric of European business and culture. *Exporters will be the first to feel the protectionist bite. Distribution of wholly foreign-made products will lose its competitive position by fiat.* Only those firms with a strong local identity, either through partnership or significant local employment, will be able to take full advantage of Europe's growing Single Market.

It Takes Two to Tango

The United States propogates its fair share of protectionism while decrying that of Europe. Foreign investment in the U.S. jumped 636 percent from $89 billion in 1980 to $401 billion in 1990.[2] A 1990 government report said that 92 percent of American manufacturing of silicon wafers is controlled by foreign firms. Representative Doug Walgren (D-PA) said in mid-1990 that 13 percent of the American manufacturing base was already foreign-owned. As a direct result, twenty-one bills were introduced in Congress that year to impose higher taxes and protectionist measures.

The protectionist voice is likely to become more shrill. Says Rimmer de Vries, Managing Director of Morgan Guarantee Trust Company, "Free capital and free trade make rare and uneasy bedfellows. "Today we may have freedom of capital flows, but the U.S. is constantly backtracking on freedom of trade."[3]

Free-traders will quickly learn that while *starting from a vastly more protectionist base, Europe is likely to follow an even more exaggerated and unpredictable course.*

10 Learning from the Experiences of Large Companies in the New Europe

M any of the larger, multinational American and European companies refer to the completion of the European Single Market as a "Non-Event."

The adjustment of the well endowed, global industrial firm to a changing Europe has been evolutionary, not revolutionary. General Electric, for example, has compelled host countries to accept it through the force of its employment and investment activities. GE's long-standing joint ventures have opened local markets and made it a familiar partner of European industry and government (as is evidenced by a recent joint venture with the French government-owned jet engine maker, Snecma).

Corporate Evolution

Dr. H. Wolff, advisor to the German government and economist with the consulting firm of Prognos AG in Basel, Switzerland, points to the global strategies of two major European electronic companies, IBM and Siemens, as examples of corporate evolution.

Why are we calling IBM a European company? With over 100,000 European employees, direction from European managers, and acceptance by its competitors as a European peer, IBM is in many ways more European than Siemens, a company still closely tied to its German roots.

Corporate Nationalism

Paternalistic and nationalistic corporate policies have historically overshadowed common sense business strategies at Siemens. While the company continues to invest in its world-wide computer business, 90 percent of its computer sales remain in Europe. To many, it is clear that the company is simply unable to compete internationally in this field. Classic Siemens paternalism manifests itself in personnel costs amounting to over 43 percent of sales (1989)—60 percent higher than those of General Electric in the U.S.—while worker lay-offs are almost unheard of. As a result, Siemens has the largest payroll in Europe with over 370,000 employees.

Like many European companies (German companies in particular), Siemens is family controlled. It carefully protects over 300 business units, only one- third of which are strongly profitable. The company is being inundated with Single Market worries.

Decontrol has threatened its historic domination of the German telecommunications equipment market. Competitive bids from suppliers elsewhere in the EC and their U.S. and Japanese partners are reducing margins substantially.

In addition, Siemens spent nearly $3 billion trying and failing to catch up to its American and Japanese semiconductor competitors.

Corporate Globalism

Meanwhile, IBM has expanded to blanket the world, producing products in hundreds of locations while becoming a truly global trading company. Its many local country plants assure cultural and political ties, yet its production from those plants is free to pursue demand beyond local borders. Guided by a central strategy, IBM seeks to maximize its production, sales, and R&D efforts on a global basis.

Is the Single Market a non-event for IBM? A 1992-inspired restructuring of the company is affecting nearly 30,000 of its workers in the EC. It is committed to increasing its customer support staff by 10,000 to meet growing local competition. While IBM holds 15 percent of Europe's total information technology market, its service and customer-driven product and market approach is out of character for Europe, especially in Germany, where the failed, Nixdorf, "black-box technology" approach has been the norm.

The Siemens philosophy had, until recently, been to cultivate acceptance in a host country as a local operative. International policy was built on a stepwise basis, leaving a group of "regional kingdoms" in its wake. Only in the last ten years has Siemens begun to evolve into a global company with a central strategy.

Recent actions are an admission by Siemens that the company cannot globalize on its own and must travel in the wake of IBM and others to assure success. Siemens took action in response to its failure in semiconductors by arranging a joint venture with IBM to develop 64 megabit memory chips. Co-development of the DRAM's by 1994 will allow a reduction in the usual time- to-market while solidifying a buyer/supplier relationship by the companies that had been in negotiations for eighteen months. While facing cash requirements of $1 billion for the project, Siemens will cement its position as second source to IBM-Europe.

At the same time, Siemens began developing an offensive telecommunications strategy. Siemens purchased IBM's Rolm division and concurrently arranged a marketing joint venture.

Its joint takeover of Plessey with GEC launched Siemens into the British telecommunications and defense markets. This flurry of activity came on the heels of the company's October, 1989, restructuring. Reconfiguring itself as a group of fifteen autonomous units, with decentralized research and cost accountability, Siemens began opening up to the outside world. For example, competition was created for executive positions. Headhunters were employed to bring in outside managers. A formal incentive program was created for young managers. While the company continues to focus on engineering research and quality, it is poised to become more market driven.

Multinationals Drive Europe Toward Unification

Dr. Wolff points out that large foreign companies have been investing in Europe for years. *Constantly looking for new markets in order to achieve greater economies of scale in both manufacturing and development, the large companies have forced a dynamic that has driven the EC toward unification.* Joint ventures among strategic competitors occur both in response to and in anticipation of the changing market place. Recent alliances between United Technologies and Daimler-Benz (investing in one another's jet engine companies) and General Electric, Thomson, and Philips (to develop high definition television) are examples of both the European action and reaction.

The Gray Line Between Competition and Cooperation

In their haste to ally, some companies rationalize away points of competitive friction. National Semiconductor and SGS-Thomson Microelectronics have a five year agreement to explore new research and development fields, and yet, they compete in the same product lines. Nevertheless, Thomson will not admit that its research partner is in its class as a global competitor.

The Eureka EU95 HDTV Project was organized in response to technology developments outside of the EC. Philips and Thomson participated in research with thirty other companies and then created a $3.6 billion joint venture of their own concentrating on system components.

It is typical for the outsider to react to changing conditions first, and only later for those within (the EC in this case) to respond. The non-EC Europeans, like Volvo, as well as the Japanese and the Americans, took the first steps toward recognition of the coming single market. These steps generated the momentum embodied by structural change—change propagated by the bureaucracy in Brussels. Formal change was later mirrored by the evolution of EC companies themselves.

The Scandinavian Foothold

Spawned in remote, small markets, Scandinavian businesses were quick to see Single Market advantages and took early steps to gain a foothold in the Community.

Ericsson (Sweden) has positioned itself in the EC telecommunications business in much the same way that fellow outsider Volvo has in the automotive market. The company has ingratiated itself to EC suppliers while simultaneously bidding for Community contracts.

Ericsson has methodically planned its alliances. The company spent eighteen months evaluating and then choosing a supplier for its printed circuit board, automatic test equipment before finally settling on Montrouge (a French division of Schlumberger) over Americans Hewlett Packard, Teradyne, and GenRad. While the automatic test equipment manufacturers are fighting tooth and nail over the European telecommunications test market (the European telecommunications equipment market is growing at 8.5 percent annually), Ericsson exploits its strategic advantages to attract the best partners. It offers its supplier a very attractive partner. Its telecom switch, the AXE, is manufactured in locations all over the world, leaving the chosen supplier a ready-made international distribution network.

While Schlumberger will use its new partnership with Ericsson to accumulate knowledge of the test and foreign markets, Ericsson will benefit in three ways:

- The company will use the alliance to share new product development costs.

- It will give Europe the faster and cheaper test methods demanded by the 1991 deadline for a pan-European digital network.

- Ericsson will solidify its position as an EC insider while globally standardizing its test products.[1]

Adapting Strategy to Pan-European Competition

American electrical connector manufacturers also entered the European market well in advance of Single Market legislation. Their successful pan-European activities have contributed to the Single Market's momentum.

As Europe's largest electrical connector supplier, AMP has three production facilities in Germany and six elsewhere in Europe. Europe's second largest supplier, ITT, is also an American-based firm. Molex, of suburban Chicago, has five European plants, whose primary function is to service the needs of Japanese companies that are now locating in Europe. The connector market is an intensely competitive one in the U.K. and Germany. While volume grew at nearly 10 percent per annum in the late 1980s, price competition held dollar growth to only 4 percent per year.

Escalating competition means a new emphasis on both service and special products. For the first time, manufacturers are shipping parts on consignment to many local markets in order to satisfy customer demands for timely delivery. In an attempt to capture a bigger piece of the Italian market, Augat stocked its Milan sales office with inventory and has doubled the staff. With European sales of $25 million, Augat has invested $4 million in a plant in England while it looks for additional European acquisitions. In this quest to make itself into a European company, it has also invested over one million dollars in a new customer management information system.

New market participants are careful to target the fastest growing segments of the connector field, just as they would in any other. For this reason, fiberoptics has become the special technology focus within the connector field. That segment of the market may reach $136 million by 1992 (Elsevier forecast), with the fastest growth within data communications (24 percent per year).

Small Competitors Must Adapt to Large Customer Needs

Though some smaller companies may also see the Single Market as a non-event, customer/supplier relationships may change based on customer adaptation to Europe's new reality. Those who supply larger, Siemens-style regional kingdoms will see market shares reduced and profitability slipping away. Those who cannot adapt to a centralizing of pan-European strategy will die in the intensely competitive regional markets.

For the smaller company, this change is revolutionary. The company must quickly grasp that all of its regional competitors may well become international competitors, each strengthened by a challenge in each of its European markets—beginning at home. Rationalization of production and distribution must take place; sales representation and personnel issues must be dealt with.

Globalizing a Niche

In this era of specialized, high-technology investment goods, markets have become increasingly international. One's actual market may have been reduced to a relatively few customers. The number of potential customers are so few, and investment in development often so large, that sales efforts must be made in every possible geographic market in order to make the investment pay off.

The strategy for the regional, niche players—whether European or American—is often three-fold:

- become global so that your special niche represents a significant absolute market,

- diversify the range of products offered in order to broaden market impact and sales potential, and

- master a single technology, or service methodology, much as Pall or ASM (as described below) have done.

Pall Corporation, selling a new blood transfusion filter, has accumulated 60 percent of its sales overseas. European breweries and wineries are using its filters to get rid of yeast and bacteria in their processing plants. Pall serves its foreign customers by making 75 percent of these overseas sales in its own plants in Europe. The company has extended the product's application and brought production and service to the customer's door.

Smaller companies have been able to successfully focus on niches in the European semiconductor markets as well. While it represents only a small part of the world's overall semiconductor consumption (8.6 percent in 1989 according to VLSI Research), growth of the European share of the world market will develop out of a niche strategy that is looking for global markets.

Advanced Semiconductor Materials International N.V. (The Netherlands) already has a global profile based on its prominence as the world's largest chemical vapor deposition system supplier. The firm keeps a low profile, but has chosen to invest in manufacturing facilities in its strongest markets (the Netherlands, Hong Kong, Japan, and the U.S.)—markets where the semiconductors are produced. To stay ahead of increasingly global competition, ASM is introducing new products while selling subsidiaries in the U.S. that are not instrumental to its primary product strategy.

Such niche-product makers are simply responding to customer behavior. *A client's internationalization frequently dictates that of the supplier.* In order to continue to serve a client or customer, the local firm is forced to find partners around the world with a high degree of special knowledge. Small German firms historically have been loathe to do this for fear of giving away a proprietary domestic edge. Small Japanese companies don't go abroad at all. They form their alliances at home. Smaller American companies have always gone directly abroad, at least initially through the use of sales representatives. However, an inability to service the European customer from a North American base has always been used as an effective competitive argument by European vendors.

The Subtle Changes at Endress & Hauser

Even where the Single Market appears to be a nonevent, subtle changes in operating strategy are being implemented. Peter Wetzer, Director of Marketing for sensors manufacturer, Endress & Hauser, emphasizes that E&H is already operating all over Europe and that its captive distributors are the "local partners" of the industries that they supply.

At the same time, rumblings over pricing are coming from large, pan-European customers. Dow Chemical, for example, has the ability to source its supplies centrally from the lowest cost countries in Europe. E&H prices have traditionally been lower in Germany than in France so that a highly professional buying approach on the part of the customer could cut E&H margins. While a small part of this country-by-country price difference may be justified by varied costs of distribution, it may represent only one- third of an 18 percent regional price differential.

At the same time, E&H is feeling the pressure from its larger customers who want to, and now have the opportunity to, reduce the number of suppliers of like parts. Rather than buy parts from suppliers in each of its local European operating areas, Dow can buy centrally, minimizing the number of suppliers, maximizing cost savings, and improving service and attentiveness on the part of the vendor selected.

Currency swings play a large part in the bottom line of an international company. Excessive fluctuation between the dollar and deutsche mark, for instance, can mean at best, translation headaches, and at worst, significant losses when costs are calculated in a local currency and sales in a foreign currency. E&H actually moved an entire product group to the U.S. in 1990 for currency reasons. The company can now sell in the U.S. for dollars while selling to all other E&H operations in Deutsche marks (DM).

Taking Advantage of Financial Deregulation

European Monetary Union or no, Monsanto is taking advantage of the European Community's financial deregulation to reduce its operating costs. It has instituted a cross-border, cash-pooling system which is allowing the company to save more than $800,000 in bank charges, interest, and foreign exchange costs.[2]

Monsanto has been a pan-European company for many years, manufacturing chemicals in Belgium and the United Kingdom and positioning sales offices in every major market. While raw materials for those European plants are purchased throughout the world, the invoices received by Monsanto are denominated in a variety of local currencies. To this panoply of cross-currency paper work, are added credit extensions that are granted by the local sales offices.

Before the financial deregulation brought about by the completion of the Single Market, convoluted commercial transactions were the norm. In Belgium, for example, local residents could not borrow French francs from nonresidents, while French laws did not allow the borrowing of French francs by nonresidents. Such restrictions forced Monsanto to close out its long and short currency positions every month. However, during the month, the Belgian manufacturing operation had interest expenses, while the French sales office received interest on its deposits. Frequently, both sides of this business were conducted at a single bank—a bank which profited from both ends of each transaction. "Now we no longer have to pay a bank to borrow our own money!" Brian Hill, Monsanto's director of banking and foreign exchange. Today, two pools, one at a domestic bank for collection and disbursements, and a second, for cross-border flows, take care of the situation. Even these improvements are far from perfect. Monsanto still cannot use the new system in Germany where domestic rules continue to penalize nonresidents. Cross border DM flows are held in Belgium.

Key Allies and Licensees Eliminate the Need for Manufacturing

Elliott Turbomachinery Company (Jeanette, PA), spun off by United Technologies and taken private in a leveraged buyout in 1987, took advantage of a recapitalization in 1989 to eliminate its currency risk. The company closed its inefficient European plants, cut staff and instituted a policy of internationalization through licensing.

Having highly engineered and customized products made licensing an easy path to pursue. Adding to the strategic beauty of the new arrangement was Elliott's link with new shareholders Ebara Corporation (Japan) and MAN Gutehoffnungshutte (Germany), participants in its 1989 recapitalization. The new minority shareholders gave the company the potential for cross-licensing, as well as proximity to international customers in both Europe and Asia. Elliott managed to eliminate currency risk while developing an international manufacturing and service program—without an investment on its part.

Corporate Actions Betray the Non-Event Label

So is Single Market Europe a non-event? Larger, already well-placed companies seem to be concerned, not with the concept itself, but with its competitive spin offs. Uniform pricing, customer sourcing policy, intense competition from companies choosing to join forces with former intra-EC competitors—each is a concern requiring a strategic response.

American companies have been better positioned than most Europeans to actually become "pan-European." Fiat, for example, sells 60 percent of its automobile production in Italy, while Ford has a major position in every European market.

American Express has 300 travel agencies in Europe and can take advantage of airline deregulation that will come with the completion of the Single European Market. As a consequence, American Express sees 20 percent annual growth ahead for itself in the EC. It will compete against European travel agencies—most being small and local.

Federal Express sees much the same profile for its air-parcel service, and is already growing at 80 percent annually in Europe.

Hewlett-Packard moved its worldwide personal computer headquarters from the U.S. to Grenoble, France, in 1990. PC sales for Hewlett-Packard in Europe already exceed those of the U.S. In fact, more than a third of the company's total sales revenue now comes from Europe.

International Paper took a firm stance on the European Single Market by buying three leading European paper companies in 1989—90. By acquiring Aussedat-Rey of France, Ilford Photographic Products from Ciba-Geigy of Switzerland, and Zanders Feinpapiere of West Germany, it enlarged a production network that already included facilities in the U.K., Italy, Sweden, Spain, and the Netherlands. Its Zanders acquisition was the ideal reciprocal combination. Its superbly efficient paper mill is in the special niche of high quality coated papers for brochures and annual reports and the like. International Paper (IP) can turn around and use this technology to enter that same market niche in the U.S. In contrast to IP, Scott Paper and Kimberly-Clark have chosen to focus on building new facilities in Europe rather than on acquisitions.

Acquiring the "European" Label

VLSI Technology not only recognizes Europe as a strategic market, but also understands the significance of being seen as a European firm with local manufacturing. This is an approach being taken by an increasing number of U.S. high technology firms. The Zehntel System Division of Teradyne has gone so far as to open a European engineering development center in the U.K. in order to give its European customers special hardware and software solutions.

VLSI, a producer of application specific integrated circuits, has its European headquarters in Munich, Germany. While its sales increased 50 percent in 1989, VLSI has made it clear that it wants to make at least 20 percent of all its products in Europe by the completion of the Single Market. It is betting that closer European customer contact in the high growth telecommunications and data processing fields will help to sever old customer/supplier relationships.

VLSI wants to exploit its U.S. technology edge and wants to do so with design engineering centers and an R&D center in France that prepares customized applications. These technology and service advantages are allowing VLSI to charge a 10 percent to 20 percent premium over competitive products.

Such strategy depends heavily on the expectation of a growing European market for ASIC's. Even with price erosion in this product segment of nearly 15 percent per year, the market is expected to double between 1990 and 1994 to over $1 billion. Nevertheless, the company will not depend on the market to dictate its growth. An alliance with Philips lets VLSI use Philips' German plant to produce some of its integrated circuits while the companies work together to develop new software tools.[3]

The Colgate-Palmolive Company is often thought of as an also-ran to Procter and Gamble in the U.S. After all, its overall revenues are just a quarter of those of its larger competitor. However, 70 percent of Colgate's sales come from abroad (vs. 40 percent for Procter and Gamble). Thirty one percent of Colgate's 1989 sales came from Europe, and even greater growth is expected due to its effective positioning there. In 1989, Colgate formed a $90 million joint venture to market household products in Portugal, and a $220 million joint venture in Italy to sell soaps and lotions—all part of a plan to buy existing credibility and distribution in new and growing markets.

The chemical process industries were active in acquiring European positions in the late 1980s in order to create a stronger base of operations for the Single Market. 3M purchased Spontex (France) to penetrate the European household and commercial cleaning product market. Air Products and Chemicals acquired Anchor Chemicals (U.K.) as its first manufacturing operation in Europe. Until that time, its European sales were exclusively exports. Earlier in the 1980s PPG made several European acquisitions in its coatings and resins businesses. W.R. Grace acquired and set up specialty chemical operations in Germany, France, and Spain in preparation for 1992. (While Monsanto, Dow, and Exxon are nearly self-sufficient in Europe, Union Carbide and even Dupont rely heavily on exports from the U.S. In fact, imports accounted for 35 percent of Dupont's sales in Europe in 1989.)

Using the New Europe to Push Diversification

Computer Sciences Corporation (El Segundo, CA), dependent on the U.S. government for a large portion of its revenues for many years, campaigned aggressively to expand to Europe and capitalize on newly deregulated data communications markets. The company created a new entity in Europe—a joint venture among itself and several European telecommunication agencies (PTT's). After two years of negotiations Infonet became a partnership of Computer Sciences and Transpac (France, 15 percent), Deutsche Bundesposte (Germany, 15 percent), Teleinvest-AB (Sweden, 5 percent), Regie des Telegraphes et des Telephones de Belgique (Belgium, 5 percent) and Compania Telefonica National de Espana SA (Spain, 5 percent). Infonet's selling point is its ability to allow customers to send information across European national borders without having to worry about changing national carriers in doing so. At the same time, Infonet counters the strength of both IBM and Electronic Data Systems in their attempts to win the battle for European value-added markets. The Bundespost and its Infonet partners can now offer their customers "one stop shopping" for all of their telecommunications needs.

In spite of all of this activity, too many large American companies do think of the Single Market as a non-event. That can be the only conclusion drawn from the statistics. According to Securities Data Company, there was a spurt of European acquisitions in 1989 by the big multinational American companies. Yet, in the first half of 1990, the activity dropped precipitously. According to Thompson Swayne of Chase Manhattan Bank, London:

> "No evidence has turned up, which we were expecting, of aggressive purchases by Americans in Europe, except for select industries like automobiles. Some fairly large U.S. companies have done no research and still don't look at Europe as a market."[4]

Then, too, some large American firms have turned to Europe as something of a market of last resort. Smith Corona controlled the portable typewriter and word processor markets in the U.S. for years until a sudden downturn in consumer durable buying cut sales and profits. The company's response was to fight new Asian competition, not with a new product or market strategy, but with an anti-dumping complaint. Soon thereafter, however, the company began to look toward Europe as a potential new market. The company has targeted 25 percent of its sales for Europe, from a standing start in 1987 and 17 percent in 1989. The fulfillment of its strategy depends on the success of a distribution agreement negotiated with Philips.[5]

Learning from the Japanese

The Japanese now have a clear picture of how they must proceed in the EC as well. After earlier venturing into the U.K., the Japanese have entered Germany by searching out partners who know the local markets. In the cosmetics field, Kao purchased Goldwell; then Goldwell quickly reached an agreement with an East German distributor to market Kao products there. Nomura took a 5 percent stake in Matuschka Group, Germany's largest independent investment bank. Matsushita makes

VCR's in partnership with Bosch and electronic components in a joint venture with Siemens.

Toshiba stated in 1990 that it would begin looking for alliances with European service and software companies in order to boost its "business systems expertise" in the European markets. Mitsubishi Electric announced the construction of its first European factory—a plant in France to manufacture cellular phones, first for Europe's analog systems, and after 1992 for its new digital network. There has been no hesitation on the part of the Japanese to use local expertise and market credibility to establish a presence that, in the long term, will develop its own identity.

There are American models of this type of approach as well. The success of Apple Computer in France has focused on the stubborn individualism of the Frenchman and his attraction to the equally individualistic Macintosh computer. This confluence of culture and product has resulted in Macintosh controlling a significant part of the French business market.

Compaq Computer rose rapidly in only three years to the third position in the French personal computer market, just behind IBM and Apple. Its unique, French approach accounted for 22 percent of the company's worldwide sales in 1989. Compaq chose to position itself in France as an upscale, service oriented product. As part of this strategy, Compaq sold its machine only through high-end dealers who would offer significant service and support to their business customers. This strategy brought immediate credibility in the French business community in the mid-1980s. The more recent opening of Compaq Business Centers, not as direct selling operations but as product promotion and service centers, simply enhances the quality image that the company has sought.

In the early 1980s the French government actively undertook a "buy French" computer campaign. In spite of that, both Thomson and Matra, with no significant penetration beyond the public sector, left the business, having been seen as little more than commodity vendors when compared with IBM, Apple or, Compaq. The two French survivors, Groupe Bull (who took over Zenith Data Systems) and SMT-Goupil, continue to live off the purchases of the French government. More than one-half of the computers used by the French government and state-run French companies in 1989 bore the Groupe Bull label.

Even for the largest of companies, the New Europe is anything but a non-event. Governments recognize that the rules have changed. Even the French government could not provide a sufficiently large and profitable market to rescue its native personal computer makers without the help of market forces and intra-industry combinations. The largest of European, American and Japanese companies have restructured or reorganized as they become more global in scope and as they race to implement efficiencies as a result. The catalyst for such restructuring has been a revitalized European market—a market whose renaissance continues to spur a surge of global planning and strategy.

11 *Successful European Strategies*

A Few European Examples

Are the best strategies for European market penetration formulated by European companies? It makes sense. The magnitude of the new opportunity for business is so great that these suddenly pan-European companies are utilizing strategies that are both time-tested and un-tested. Recapturing markets that had been lost to non-European, global competitors is requiring money, imagination, and intra-industry cooperation.

Rather than attempt to duplicate the American multinational experience, European-based companies of all sizes are taking a close look at their assets and how they can best be applied close to home. Many are taking advantage of close working relationships with university research centers, of fortuitous geographic positioning, or of technical uniqueness to promote business growth and efficiency.

Firms that are outgrowths of the publicly funded research process can benefit perpetually from a relationship that provides them with staff, equipment, funding, and proprietary technology. Cobrain N.V. of

167

Belgium was founded to commercialize a dry etching process spawned from the pure research activities of the Interuniversity Microelectronic Center. Cobrain is the only firm in its field with access to the equipment and research results of an institute which is backed by government funding of $2.5 billion. Without the capital draining research that a competitor might be forced to absorb, Cobrain can address the customer's applications and provide services that might not otherwise be available. This is an invaluable advantage in so narrow a market.

The rationalization strategy of Electrotech (Bristol, England) is worth examining, given European expectations of relatively high levels of quality and service. This $50 million company had nineteen geographically spread European operating units. In the face of competition spawned by the approaching completion of the Single Market, the company underwent a streamlining process which has reduced its operating units to just one. In the process, administrative staff was cut 20 percent, and customer support staff grew by 10 percent. The company underwent a change, not only in structure, but also in philosophy—from that of a technology driven company to that of a market driven company, promoting efficiency and service.

Suppose that you have a clear technical edge over the competition? How can you exploit it? Esec, a $23 million sales Swiss semiconductor equipment manufacturer has a technological edge over its American and Japanese competitors. It specializes in die bonding equipment and has gained nearly a quarter of the world market for such equipment—a market otherwise dominated by the Japanese. Esec is ambitiously pursuing the broader wire bonding equipment market by funneling about 21 percent of every sales dollar into research and development.

Each of the company's four geographic operating divisions has the authority to act independently. This has given the company the flexibility necessary to adapt its approach to differing markets and applications. The company subcontracts the manufacturing of several models and carefully audits those subcontractors on a regular basis in order to maintain a reputation built on quality and customer service.

In the consumer products field, the completion of the Single market can mean the application of advertising and marketing methods that have been used in the U.S. for years.

Cadbury-Schweppes (U.K.) has given its European soft drink business an entirely new look in an effort to create a single European image. The company wants to exploit economies of scale and can do so only by finding common market characteristics, rather than the differences around which past regional marketing campaigns were built. Out go the separate national marketing and advertising campaigns and in comes a single European campaign.

Such a change in strategy also implies a new, broad management perspective. To implement the new strategy, Cadbury-Schweppes must bring in truly European managers from the outside.

Many foreign companies have already taken a European approach by focusing on a substantial, physical European presence in a well-defined market niche. Bandag (U.S.) gets 42 percent of its retread tire sales from abroad. It is manufacturing in Europe to protect its share of a market in which retreads account for nearly two-thirds of all truck tire sales. Mentor Graphics (U.S.) sells more than one-half of its electronic design automation systems abroad, so it has invested in research and development facilities in both Europe and Asia.

European firms have developed strategies to take advantage of changes in the financial structure of the New Europe as well. For Trans European Airways, the coming of the Single European Market was a boon to its young business. Using a Brussels hub as its niche, it built a charter airline to capitalize on coming changes in the aviation market, and in doing so, saw revenues triple to $300 million in 1989.

Trans European simultaneously built a winning financial strategy based on global tools, hedging against swings in its three greatest cost variables: the cost of energy, interest rates, and foreign exchange. Energy, for example, represents 12 percent of Trans European's cost base. Hedging through the use of futures contracts saved over $1 million in fuel costs in 1989. Swaps, options, and forward contracts were also used to hedge currency exchange rate fluctuations, an area where Trans European had a quarter of a million dollars in trading gains from currency options positions.

Because interest rates have so great an effect on the demand for travel services, forward rate agreements were used to take advantage of below market rates. In the long run, hedging gives the company the opportunity to smooth gains and losses from year to year and avoid drastic cutbacks or increases in assets or personnel throughout the business cycle.[1]

The process of expanding to Europe or expanding in Europe must begin with a feel for the lay-of-the-land. Getting to know the market place demands that time be spent with the middlemen and end-users. Unexploited niches must be found and competitors observed.

Competition is still quite new to many European industry segments. *Get a feel for how competitive you can be without being culturally insensitive.* Determine just what a new company can add to the market that isn't already there. Finally, look hard at the competition and decide who among them can best benefit from that new product, service or operating method that you bring to the market. It is rarely necessary to break new ground in the New Europe. Let the European examples—their successes and failures—point you in the right direction.

12 *Establishing the Smaller American Company in Europe*

Alternatives

How much does it cost to establish one's relatively small American business in the New Europe? The answer is dependent on one's needs, time horizon, resources, and strategy. Here are six methods, in very simplified form, used to get up and running, listed in ascending order of their implementation cost:

1. *Send a company staffer to Europe for two weeks to find a customer.* This approach can cost as little as a few thousand dollars for transportation and accommodations. Any continuing operating costs are associated with occasional visits and contacts with the client and with the possible modification of a product or service to meet European technical or service

standards. But, do you repeat this process each time you look for a new order?

2. *Export your product to customers who have learned about it through an independent resource* (such as a catalog, an embassy listing, a trade show, or advertisement). Your investment is in the advertising medium and trade arrangement as well as in travel needed to service that customer. Once having secured a customer, continuing operating costs are as in #1 above.

3. *Organize a joint venture with a local European partner.* Now you are beginning to talk about serious money. A European company that is both interested in working with you and yet brings some substantial advantages of its own to the table, will be found only through diligent research—conducted by your in-house staff or by an outside European consultant. Once underway, the venture's cost is borne by both partners, as is the benefit. Once a suitable partner is found, he will want to see a commitment from you to the partnership, so be prepared to put your money where your mouth is.

4. *Set up a company, starting from scratch, and stock it with American personnel*, at least at the management level. While this is an expensive way to be introduced to the market place, it allows for nearly complete control of all operations in what otherwise might be too geographically distant a market.

5. *Set up a company, starting from scratch, and stock it with local workers.* A business is less costly to run with local managers who are comfortable in the local business environment than it is with imported and trained Americans who will have to interact with an unfamiliar culture.

6. *Acquire an existing local company.* While likely to be the most expensive of the alternatives listed in the short-term, it may be more efficient in the long run and be less expensive than starting a company from

scratch, hiring new staff, promoting one's product to a new market, and manufacturing or delivering a product from a remote location. Adding your own logo and brand name to an existing line brings rapid acceptance and credibility—whether done through acquisition or joint venture.

Applying Theory to Practice

Whatever the strategy chosen and whatever the cost, no European expansion will proceed precisely along the lines of another. Each product or service has its own appeal, and each distribution network has its own special composition. The six alternatives listed above are broad categories within which to work and plan. However, a good deal of creativity can be brought to bear on the process.

Getting Creative

Creative strategies that may spell success in one European market may not carry the day in neighboring markets. The strong sense of mission that often accompanies technology leadership led one of the relatively early leaders in the development of computer hardware for artificial intelligence applications—Syntech[1]—to look at international expansion. Being relatively new, with American markets immature but growing, the company found a real need to spread its development costs over a wider customer base. Europe, while even less mature in its level of demand for this type of equipment, was still a sophisticated technological market with significant long-term sales potential.

Seeing few competitive barriers to entry standing in its path in Western Europe, Syntech chose to set up shop in Frankfurt, Germany, in order to be near that country's industrial base. The newly established German subsidiary took on the typical private limited liability, corporate designation of GmbH (Gesellschaft mit beschrankter). The subsidiary grew and prospered, becoming a strong presence in German industry.

With success in hand, it seemed intuitively obvious that expansion elsewhere in Europe was indicated. Seeking to build on its German language facility and success, Syntech established a second subsidiary in Zurich, Switzerland, in order to open up a market which, though small in absolute numbers of companies, was the home of several of the largest industrial firms in Europe. After two years of trying, Syntec simply closed up shop in Switzerland and retreated quietly to Germany with its tail tucked snuggly between its legs. What happened?

Syntec chose not to tamper with its successful German formula. Its Swiss organization was, for reporting purposes, absorbed by its German progenitor. Its products were imported from the German unit, and generally in final form, so that only limited customization could be done in the proximity of the customer. In addition, the Swiss subsidiary was organized, for legal and financial reasons, as GmbH rather than as the typical Swiss AG (Aktiengesellschaft/Ltd./stock corporation). It seems that some Swiss are not fond of the Germans (be careful where you drive your big Mercedes in Switzerland), and that the GmbH in Switzerland carries a number of negative connotations—often because it is neither well known nor understood. To many, the German suffix was simply an indication that this firm was a foreign company with little local credibility.

Palo Alto-based ABC Corporation is in the business of developing and marketing mainframe expert system development tools. As one of the first AI firms to offer an expert systems tool for an IBM mainframe running in a particular operating environment, ABC developed a growth strategy based on sales to software firms who would use the ABC product to develop a variety of application products. They successfully sold their system to many applications software developers, including Boole & Babbage, Management Science America, Arthur Andersen Consulting, and others. Testifying to the success of this strategy was the fact that IBM itself chose, in certain markets, to promote this third-party product rather than its own competing product.

Without a foreign expansion strategy in place, ABC stumbled successfully into the German market. A German subsidiary of a global bank used the ABC product in its development of an internal expert system. In an attempt to capitalize on this first expert system success in the IBM operating environment, ABC sought a German-based software distributor to handle its product. While expertise in AI and breadth of distribution were clearly major considerations in this search, ABC ultimately settled on a distributor whose greatest advantage was its close ties to a major American ABC customer. Without a strong basis in expert systems hardware and software, the new distributor was neither able to properly demonstrate nor service the ABC product. The distributor actually engaged an outside AI expert to demonstrate the ABC product to potential customers.

Meanwhile, with the passing of time, ABC began to lose the edge that had been built on its initial product success. An American competitor, DEF Corp., jumped at the chance to fill the void. *DEF, seeing Germany as one of several regional opportunities but understanding the need to address each locally with local staff, began seeking European venture capital with which to create locally owned DEF subsidiaries in each national market.* After establishing its European headquarters in the Netherlands, DEF built subsidiaries in Germany and France, manned by local managers and owners. The market advantage once held by ABC was gone. Prodded into action, it finally abandoned its representation and established its own subsidiary in Cologne. ABC now shares the IBM mainframe expert systems market with at least four others, some with considerably greater financial resources with which to wage the battle.

Viewlogic Systems Inc. of Marlboro, Massachusetts,[2] is following a similarly creative strategy in order to grab a bigger piece of the European computer-aided engineering (CAE) design tool market. The $20 million company competes directly with the much larger Mentor Graphics, Valid Logic Systems, and Daisy Systems, all of whom have well established European direct sales operations. While its competitors are growing in Europe at a rapid pace, Viewlogic sales there peaked out at only 14 percent of overall company sales. With a corporate goal of 25 percent of sales, and in the face of an expected public offering of stock in the U.S., Viewlogic needed to find a strategy for European expansion that was both effective and insulated from the American public offering.

After eighteen months of negotiations, Viewlogic Europe BV, headquartered at The Hague, was launched. This independent European company was financed with $4.5 million of exclusively European venture capital. Viewlogic retained only 20 percent of the equity in its European namesake. However, if and when sales hit a predetermined level, a one-to-one stock swap with the U.S. parent will be activated, based upon a successful U.S. public offering. When the European company becomes profitable, Viewlogic will acquire the company in a stock swap.

In developing the venture capital financing strategy, View logic sought only investors from its key European markets: France, Germany, and the U.K. Losses from the start-up had to be kept off the financial statements of the American parent in order to prevent interference with the American public offering.

Viewlogic had previously marketed in Europe through a single distribution chain. With sales never reaching expectations, and heavy technical support required for its products, the company opted for its venture capital-backed approach. Company plans now include:

- a direct sales force managed by European headquarters,

- sales offices in the U.K., Germany, France, and Italy,

- seven continental sales teams, each comprising one salesman and one engineer,

- a Netherlands manufacturing and distribution base,

- a training center in its old U.K. sales office,

- a European OEM liaison, and

- agreements with Plessey Semiconductors and SGS-Thomson to bundle Viewlogic tools with their software packages.

Building on Success

One of the highest quality artificial intelligence tools available is a piece of software produced and sold by Brainchild Corp. in North America. The company's ability to sell and develop this AI tool in the U.S. was reason to begin looking at Europe as a secondary market. The technological sophistication and market opportunity of West Germany was as attractive to Brainchild as it was to Syntech above.

A European headquarters was established in Munich, and an American manager was sent over from the company's California home base. The company, either through dumb luck or careful analysis, had chosen a perfect European manager to both start up and run the operation. This manager had an unusual interest in Europeans and their cultures, and although he did not speak German initially, within a few months he was making product presentations in that language, further ingratiating himself to the local market. Management back in California had the good sense to give this manager a great deal of operating freedom—freedom that was translated into a long list of new customers. While the branch offices or subsidiaries of other American firms were busy overseeing each and every regional office expenditure, Brainchild gave its man the freedom to run a business according to local needs.

Brainchild's manager was unusually successful in fighting off the German forays of other American firms. For example, an American competitor chose to enter the German market through a joint distribution venture with a well-known British technology firm. However, the approaches by English speaking sales people and applications engineers paled by comparison to the home-grown response of Brainchild. As its growth pattern became well established in Germany, Brainchild transferred this manager back to the States where he set about rebuilding a domestic territory. Meanwhile, a new German general manager was chosen who could build on the existing sensitivity to the nuances of German culture. Market share continued to grow as further expansion within Europe was planned, based on the German model.

Planned Success

It was not the struggle of the typical American entrepreneur, but perhaps it is for that reason that a group of professional managers was able to design and implement a plan as envisioned. Intelligencia Corp. developed and successfully marketed two very high level expert systems, primarily for use in the banking and insurance industries.

With a board full of experienced venture capitalists, Intelligencia plotted a strategy that would spread world-wide the very significant cost of application development over banks, insurance companies, and their centers of concentration. Recognizing London as just such a center, Intelligencia moved quickly to find a large insurance company in Britain with whom it could jointly develop the product's application and markets.

After successfully installing its product at one of the largest U.K. insurers, Intelligencia and the insurer put together a separate, shared-ownership joint venture, in which the insurer has majority ownership and exercises its European experience in changing the marketing and sales strategy. This international joint-venture is now contracting with highly experienced AI firms on the Continent for distribution and service of the Intelligencia products on a region-by-region basis.

"Small" Means "Flexible"

Some small companies have taken advantage of their unusual technology or lack of sufficient American market opportunity to become European market players. Security Tag Systems, Inc (STS)., a small St. Petersburg, Florida, company[3] went to Europe in 1982 by way of a joint venture partner. While the company used direct sales representatives in the U.S., it was willing to give up part of its profit margin to a joint venture partner, but not as much as would have been taken by a European distributor. STS and Automated Security Holdings of London set up a U.K. joint venture company that purchases product from STS in Florida and sells to its European clientele.

Medical Graphics Corporation of St. Paul, Minnesota, an $11 million maker of medical diagnostic equipment generates 30 percent of its business from international activities. After three years of working through a distributorship in West Germany, the company has opened a single man, direct sales office both to replace the distributor and to let the market know that it is serious about the German market.

FlowMole Corporation of Kent, Washington, a $40 million company specializing in the obscure microtunneling business, was forced to look at Europe because of the slow development of business in the U.S.[4] The company both succeeded and failed there with two different operating strategies.

FlowMole was able to generate European interest in its technology by arranging demonstrations for public utility companies in the U.K., The Netherlands, and Germany. These meetings led to both contracts and licensing agreements. Where licensing took place (in Belgium, The Netherlands, and Germany), the company was able to train a carefully selected local contractor and generate revenue by leasing him equipment, collecting royalties, and selling him spare parts. In the U.K., the company chose to directly solicit and fill customer contracts.

In doing so, it lost nearly $1 million over the course of a year of operations, and later opted to change its strategy to the more successful licensing strategy pursued on the continent.

The smaller American company is likely to have a significant advantage over the larger industrial firm when seeking to enter or expand in the New Europe. Flexibility and an ability to be overlooked by both the regulators and larger Continental competition can allow the smaller American firm to set up shop and do an effective analysis of its market opportunities. It is at that point that the firm can begin to take a hard look at both joint venture and merger partners in the hope of capitalizing on that opportunity.

IV
EASTERN (CENTRAL) EUROPE

13

The New Eastern Europe: Opportunity or Trap

P arallels are often drawn between contemporary Eastern Europe and post-World War II Western Europe. It took Western Europe a decade to re-build after the destruction of the war. Its new governments and shattered institutions were forced to deal with valueless currencies, food rationing, and barter-based economies as well as with millions of refugees—the products of destroyed homes and broken lives. The Marshall Plan, economic restructuring, and political stability used the strong European work ethic as a springboard to economic renaissance.

Central Europe has undergone a similar shock with a comparable degree of destruction. The destructive powers of corrupt state-Socialism left these nations mired in the past, unable to develop their infrastructures, economies, or standards of living. The sudden fall of a series of economically, socially, and politically repressive regimes brought a sudden end to a decrepit, dysfunctional, institutional charade.

The Economic Reality

Industrial output in Central Europe is falling dramatically. In 1989—90, declines of 3 percent, 9 percent, 11 percent and 28 percent were registered in Czechoslovakia, Hungary and Bulgaria, Yugoslavia, Romania and Poland respectively.[1] The region entered 1991 having to pay real market rates and real money for its energy, while its historic supplier, the U.S.S.R., was forced to cut back supplies. It was estimated that Czechoslovakia would spend more than 90 percent of all hard currency export earnings on oil in 1991. For Bulgaria and Poland those figures would be 120 percent and 40 percent.

The "sugar daddy" relationship that the Soviet Union had with its satellites is a thing of the past. The Soviet economy shrank by 3 percent in 1990 and lost 50 percent of its record harvest to waste (Figure 28 and 29). Housing is not available. A nascent environmental

FIGURE 28:   EUROPEAN ECONOMIC REALITY

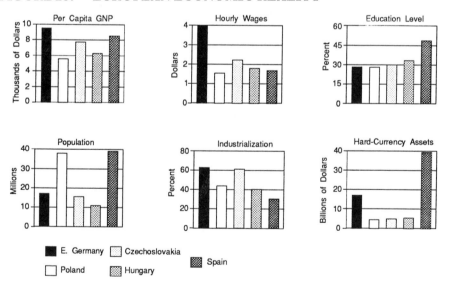

Source: EC, Plan Econ

**FIGURE 29:   EAST/WEST CONTRAST: A 1988 COMPARISON OF THE
TWO GERMANIES**

	W. Germany	E. Germany
Gross Income in Industry in bn DM/Marks (mo.)	3,657	1,292
Disposable Income p.c. and month DM/Marks	1,814	813
Savings Rate	13.9%	7.0%
Money Volume in bn DM/Marks	143	15.6
Financial Assets p.c. in DM/Marks	40,747	11,022
Durable Consumer Goods in % Households		
–Automobiles	97	52
–Color TV	94	52
–Telephone	98	8
–Deep Freezers	77	43
Apartments p.c. in m^2	35.5	27.0
Apartments with Baths in %	98	72

Source: Swiss Bank Corporation

movement has blocked Occidental Petroleum and Montedison from establishing Soviet petrochemical projects. The struggle between Moscow and the republics for control of natural resources and economic change could become dangerously disruptive at any time. The Moscow News predicted in late 1990 that as many as 8 million Soviets would soon try to leave in response to deteriorating economic conditions. Their likely destination: Western Europe.[2]

The long and gradual economic decline imposed on the Central European states left in its wake as many as three generations of economically disabled citizens. The contemporary Central European mindset is in many ways diametrically opposite that of the West. The task at hand is not simply one of rebuilding and retraining, as was the case in Western Europe after WWII, but one of the "spiritual reorientation" of millions of workers who have had economic risk introduced into their lives for the first time. The conversion of Central Europe to something more than a ward of the Western welfare system will be a long and painful process.

The Absence of Infrastructure

The job at hand is too critical to simply drop in the hopper with the many other calls on the resources of the World Bank. Instead, a European Bank for Reconstruction has taken over this task. Twenty four Western countries have pledged eleven billion ECU. The EC made 300 million ECU available in 1990 for training and private enterprise development.

In concert with the necessary spiritual reorientation, an infrastructure neglected for fifty years must be replaced. What is it like to do business without a telephone? There are approximately 500 telephones for every 1,000 Americans, nearly the same for West Germans, but only about fourteen for every 1,000 East Germans.[3] Pay phones in Warsaw accept only one of three different sized twenty-zloty coins, which no one seems to have. A phone call from the airport to Budapest, just a twenty minute ride away, is often inaudible. Imagine being neither able to communicate by phone nor to drive across town to meet face-to-face? There are nearly 600 passenger cars for every 1,000 Americans, but only eleven for every 1,000 Czechs. Heavy rains can make large portions of Warsaw inaccessible by both road and foot.

Both individuals and businesses are handicapped by the lack of commercial and individual services. In some areas of Central Europe, checking accounts are unheard of. At GE's Tungsram light bulb factory in Hungary, workers manually stuff cash into 17,000 pay envelopes every month.

The Absence of Incentive

The Central European work ethic has been surpressed by generations of accepted inefficiency. The profit motive is unknown. Western managers have trouble finding understandable words to define and explain the nature of profit and the need for it at all. Monetary incentives for workers are all but unknown. When the Schwinn Bicycle Company took a 51 percent interest in a Hungarian factory, there was less than a 15 percent differential between the wages of the factory manager and the night watchman.

The very word, "incentive," is associated with the black market. Incentives normally accrue to low and mid-level bureaucrats whose palms need to be greased with favors and gifts in order to expedite administrative paperwork. Business ethics have been a casualty of state-controlled economies and black market commerce.

Entrepreneurship in Central Europe

The European and American philosophies differ fundamentally. Unlike Americans, both Eastern and Western European citizens were weaned on the belief that the people exist to support the state, rather than the reverse. The assertion of individual initiative and the trappings of success and reward that it may bring are disdained. Hungarian entrepreneurs, while they may benefit materially from their business ventures, are anything but admired.

The U.S. Chamber of Commerce, Center for International Private Enterprise (funded by the National Endowment for Democracy), has invested in two projects in Poland and Hungary. The Krakow Industrial Society has been granted $62,000 to train entrepreneurs and publish position papers on economic reform. The Hungarian Association of Entrepreneurs (VOSZ) was given $60,000 to develop a public information campaign on entrepreneurship. Nevertheless, entrepreneurship carries negative connotations. For example, the successful shopkeeper wife of a Hungarian bureaucrat gets little public or social credit even though her income may be many times that of her well-respected husband. Also, prior to conducting business, Polish entrepreneurs must register before administrative courts. Independent business activities are most likely to be viewed favorably if they appear to support state objectives while offering broad popular benefits.

Bright Spots in the Darkness

When Westerners look at Central Europe, they see Moscow needing a city-wide infrastructure "fix" of $6 billion in highways, housing, hotels, communications, and more. They see the shipment of ICL's computers from London to Lenningrad having to travel by boat, face delays at Russian ports, and sit for weeks awaiting government approval for passage; they see bumper crops rotting in the fields for lack of fuel and machinery to harvest them; they see inflation rates of several hundred percent as state economies introduce free market principles; and they see unworkable accounting systems making it nearly impossible to "price out" companies, properties, or entire economies.

The move toward a market or mixed economy is a double-edged sword. Eyewitness testimony supplies good reason for both optimism and depression:

> The productive assets of the (Polish) factories are good. The plant and equipment are generally adequate, though not always modern...In addition, a number of the products represent good

value from a customer's point of view. On the debit side, production is often highly inefficient. Many companies are overextended vertically. They produce some parts that they could purchase more cheaply from outside suppliers.[4]

While Polish companies now can convert currency and get outside supplies from a variety of sources, they simply do not know how to begin. After years of manufacturing based entirely on production figures, there is no concept of production cost, nor of the value of an individual component if it should need to be outsourced. No incentives for or systems of quality improvement or management exist. In what was previously a shortage economy, the need for marketing was nonexistent. Now with a contracting market, real costs and intense competition, many of these enterprises are completely paralyzed. There is no facility for market research because the now disbanded government bureaucracies handled all distribution. Few Polish companies have any idea of who needs a product or how much of it might be needed.

Central Europe's balance sheet seems to show a seriously negative net worth. But there are some promising assets. Finding these assets and nursing them back to health may be well worth the effort, even in the face of obstacles and uncertainty. The information, knowledge, and infrastructure needs of the region are incredible. The opportunity to satisfy those needs will be taken up by Western suppliers. *There may be a short-term payoff vis-a-vis Western Europe and a long-run ground floor opportunity for those who can participate in the region's rebirth.*

14 *Moving to a Market Economy*

S tructural and philosophical considerations aside, Central European economies bear a superficial resemblance to their Western counterparts. Per capita incomes in the East compare quite favorably with those of EC member states Portugal and Greece, for example.[1]

Country	per capita income
Poland	$ 5,453
Hungary	6,491
Czechoslavakia	7,603
East Germany	9,361
Portugal	3,772
Greece	4,500
West Germany	14,590

Derived from a state controlled system that no longer exists, these numbers are now almost meaningless. As is the case with Portugal and Greece, the rebuilding of Central European economies depends on their ability to draw support and know-how from new Western partners.

Getting Our Feet Wet in Central Europe

According to the U.S. Chamber of Commerce, American companies accounted for 125 of 1,500 joint ventures registered in the Soviet Union and 100 of 930 in Poland.in 1990. Thousands of state-owned businesses are being slowly privatized throughout Central Europe. As of early 1990, $500 million in private capital had been invested in 700 Hungarian joint ventures with Western firms, 190 with U.S. participation.

Hungary, furthest along on the path toward a market economy, has a private banking system that attracts Western deposits with its guarantees of extreme secrecy. There are liberal ownership and hard currency repatriation rules as well. A State Property Agency has been created to give its approval to property values and accounting valuations (which do not always agree with Western calculations). The InvestCenter in Budapest has racks of booklets (in English!) of foreign investment procedures and laws and serves a matchmaking role as well.

Austria, the closest Western country to the East both geographically and historically, sees itself as filling a needed bridging role. Nearly one-third of the joint ventures in Hungary have Austrian partners. Austria gives more per capita aid to Poland and Hungary than does any Western state. The Vienna/Budapest Worlds Fair of 1995 makes Austria an even more important and timely link.

Is it Safe to Proceed?

Whether a link to the East is established through Austria or another experienced party, choosing the friendliest national surroundings will be difficult. Czechoslovakia has the most advanced industrialized economy in Central Europe, with strong machine tool and engineering industries and little foreign debt. The Crown is a commercially convertible currency and the process of returning 70,000 pieces of nationalized property to their pre-1955 owners has begun. The government wants to privatize 70 percent of its state-owned businesses. Unfortunately, the move to a market economy is having serious repercussions. Unemployment of about 12 percent in 1990 is expected to at least double with economic reform.[2]

Hungary, while on the path toward economic liberalization, is sponsoring new legislation that may affect tax incentives that have already been given to U.S. investors. The U.S. Chamber of Commerce has a Hungarian-U.S. Business Council lobbying the Hungarian government to grandfather these incentives. Corporation law is still evolving and is subject to change at almost any time.

Poland has the advantage of having had something of an entrepreneurial history to draw on. Even during its domination by the Soviets, 80 percent of Polish agriculture was in private hands. This compares with 90 percent of Hungarian and Czech agriculture that is still controlled by the state.

Given Central Europe's needs and the consumption of its limited hard currency by its energy purchases, can Central Europe be a market for Western products? Czechoslovakia has a plan to raise its foreign programming content on its primary broadcast channel from 24 percent of its schedule to 30 percent in 1990 and 40 percent in 1991. How will it pay for that programming?

Poland spent $1.6 million on foreign programming in 1989. In a country of 38 million people and $40 billion of foreign debt, will the Polish be able to purchase any additional programming in the future?

Governments are unstable, asset ownership is unclear, language and cultural differences are formidable. Is there any reason to look East?

15 Business Strategy for Central Europe

G iven the uncertainty, risk, and miserable eco-nomic conditions, why consider doing business in Central Europe at all?

Many are convinced that they can start a profitable enterprise in Central Europe now. Sure, a few companies with special products or niches will be able to make a go of it. They may link up with one or more governments or funding agencies (World Bank, etc.) to provide a profitable product or service that can be distributed by the state. However, there are just two chances for most of us to be one of those priviledged few: slim and none. While there may be private customers in these countries, they have little convertible currency, and, you may not be able to repatriate it. Central European governments may be in worse shape than their individual consumers. For all intents and purposes, these countries are bankrupt.

This having been said, there are still two very compelling reasons to believe that you should be in Central Europe and that you should be there now:

1. *Central Europe may be your best way into Western European markets.* With many industries dominated by protectionist sentiment, meaningful American market penetration in the West may not be possible. The excluded sectors, electronics and textiles, may be good examples. If, when economic times get tough, American participation in these or other industries is restricted, then Central Europe may provide the opening that is required. Just as European firms have circumvented American protectionist measures by exporting to the U.S. from subsidiaries in Latin America or the Far East, American firms can export to Western Europe from Eastern European plants, subsidiaries, and joint ventures.

Over the next few years the EC will have signed agreements with every Central European country, each allowing special access to tis markets. Central Europe will leapfrog the U.S. and Japan and move to the center of Mr. Delors' set of *concentric circles.* What's more, unlike EFTA, Central Europe will be the beneficiary of *active* aid programs from the community which, while limiting immigration from Central Europe, will provide a market place for Central European products.

The American company that has established a presence in Central Europe and employs local workers will ultimately find a barrier-free, low labor cost road to Western markets.

2. *Lay the ground work now for real business in developing, Central European markets.* It may be ten years before Central European citizens and governments have any meaningful buying power. It may be twenty years. What would you give to have had this kind of ground floor opportunity in Western Europe forty five years ago? At some point in the not too distant future there will be meaningful markets in Central Europe for your products and services. Setting up shop and building relationships now will give American companies an opportunity to avoid the "ugly

American" label that is so frequently applied to speculators and latecomers. At this relatively early stage, an American company can position itself as an economic development aid to a struggling national economy. The risks are there, but the long-term reward can be substantial.

By combining the intent of points one and two above, Western Europe can be addressed while you accustom yourself to Eastern ways, culture, language and personnel. You can build an acceptable company profile in a place where your aggressive American approach might otherwise be poorly received.

What are the first steps to be taken in establishing and developing a business in Central Europe?

Once you know your business and have focused on market segments and gaps that look promising, you will want to do market research to confirm the presence of those gaps just as you have for Western Europe. *Forget it*. There is no good quality market research being done in these countries and you cannot afford to develop it yourself.

This being the case, just swallow your ego and begin the search for someone who has done this before:

1. *Check out some brokers.* They may call themselves Eastern European business brokers, consultants, agents, or matchmakers. You can find them in directories, in phone books, through the Commerce Department and State Department, and by word of mouth. Interview each of them and scrupulously check their credentials. Do they speak the languages of Eastern Europe? Do they know the culture? Are their contacts current (it won't help to be closely connected to a bureaucrat who is now out of power)? Can they document their claims?

2. *Let your agent (broker) lead you to joint venture and partnership candidates.* A good agent will perform his function for a finders fee and expenses. Be leery

of those who expect a retainer or bill for their time. They are simply telling you that the meter will be running while they do their homework and get up to speed. You are not interested in waiting or in paying for their education. A good agent or broker already knows the field of candidates and his familiarity with the territory means that he can turn up new ones quickly. If more incentive is needed, perhaps equity participation ought to be offered.

3. *Check out joint venture candidates as carefully as possible.* You will want to check with government and public sources of information, but put most of your effort into talking with workers, competitors, and customers. Tour the plant; wait outside at quitting time. Contact financial institutions, in Germany in particular, to see if there has been occasion in the past to check out this candidate for one of their own customers. German companies have been aggressively looking East and their bankers take more than an arms-length interest in such matters.

4. *Negotiate with every party who may have a proprietary interest in your venture.* Disputes over ownership and jurisdiction will be common over the next decade, so you may find yourself negotiating with a party that really does not own the asset you wish to share. Typical agreements in the Soviet Union may involve several joint venture partners including the State, the Republic, the municipality, and the enterprise itself. Inadvertently omitting one or more of these parties may incapacitate your venture.

5. *Look for an institutional partner to include in order to capitalize on distribution possibilities.* When Britain's ICL joint ventured with the Soviet merchant marine, it knew full well that it had both a built-in buyer and distributor for its computers. Private distribution networks are few and far between in Central Europe. As a production-based economy, the state was responsible for the distribution of whatever may have been produced. With the state's new reduced

role, many concerns are sinking, completely lacking in any marketing or distribution direction. Some state agencies still remain critical in the new economic structure. They deal with essential and sensitive sectors of the economy—telecommunications, energy, public transportation, and health, for example—and each is a potential outlet for traditional state-controlled distribution. The Soviet Union has 900,000 railroad tank cars as compared to 200,000 in the United States. Suppose it is your intention to provide service for such equipment. It might be important to have both state and republic ministries of transport as parties to your venture.

6. *Search hard for and train local management.* American firms are not going to survive in Central Europe for any length of time without having local talent involved in the management of these enterprises. General Electric was fortunate to already have a Hungarian-born, American-trained manager on staff when it acquired a controlling interest in a Hungarian light bulb maker. Few companies will be so fortunate to find individuals who are familiar with the local language and culture, and who also understand American management techniques and concepts. Managers are in short supply in the East, and the requirements and pressures imposed by a system composed of companies each with several hundred employees but only a single telephone are very special indeed.

7. *Take advantage of cheap labor and cost effective R & D in Central Europe where applicable.* Average Polish wages are between $50 and $100 a month. In GE's Hungarian light bulb plant, labor cost is only 25 percent of production cost as compared to 50 percent in the U.S. This is clearly one of the reasons the automotive companies have so actively pursued Central European plants and locations. Central European workers are very technical. Basic, long-term research has been carried out for years without the

pressure brought to bear by cost and profitability concerns. Each of the Eastern countries seems to have an area of strength that can be tapped for comparatively little. The U.S.S.R. is strong in composite materials, Poland in system control engineering, and Czechoslovakia and Hungary in manufacturing technology. Babcox and Wilcox has $100,000 invested in research at the Budapest Technical University. Monsanto and the Soviet Academy of Sciences are doing basic research in bioorganic chemistry.[1]

8. *Take advantage of special investment incentives and banking arrangements.* Every Eastern country has developed or is in the process of developing a set of special investment incentives for foreign firms. Tax holidays are common. Real estate and industrial plants are often donated to the overall effort. Take in the government or agency as a partner and all sorts of goodies can be added.

Financing your venture may be considerably more difficult. Allergic to uncertainty, banks are reluctant to provide loans for anything more than a year in Central Europe. In addition, a bank typically will demand a guarantee from the Western partner. Several U.S. government programs may be useful here. The Agency for International Development (AID), the Foreign Credit Insurance Association, and the Export-Import Bank can all take a hand in this effort. The Ex-Im Bank now has a $200 million term loan facility available. Loans of this type will have guarantees against expropriation and the inconvertibility of currency, too.

OPIC, the Overseas Private Investment Corporation (Washington, DC), offers political risk insurance, loan guarantees, and direct loans for from five to twelve years to American operations in developing countries. Poland, Hungary, Yugoslavia, and Czechoslovakia now qualify. Inconvertibility coverage is also offered. General Electric, for example, has $100 million of such risk insurance covering its

Tungsram investment. Depending on the political risk factors, annual premiums range from 0.2 percent to 2.5 percent of an investment.

The next section of the book demonstrates how some companies have ventured into Central Europe, attempting to make the best of the short-term while positioning themselves for the long haul.

16

A Foothold in the East

Eastern Investments Provide a Western Competitive Edge

Several large multinationals have grandiose plans and great expectations for the rapidly evolving Central European states. Fiat proposes to use these newly "freed" economies as a base for pan-European expansion. With a desire to lower production costs and to prepare for an explosion of pent-up demand, the company plans to build 900,000 cars annually in Eastern Europe by 1996. In February 1990 it took the first steps along this path by completing a joint venture agreement with Poland's FSM Automobile Company to build subcompact cars and export 50,000 to Western Europe in 1991.

General Motors, through its Adam Opel subsidiary, wants to produce 150,000 units in East Germany and take advantage of the same cost advantages and latent market demand as Volkswagen and Mercedes. GM also has a joint venture in Hungary with RABA (trucks, diesel engines), and paid $150 million for two-thirds of a production plant venture near the Austrian border.[1]

Using Barter to Establish Market Presence

In response to Pepsico's dominance of the Central European soft drink market, Coke has joint ventured for the purpose of initiating distribution throughout the former Eastern Block. Previously available only through hard currency stores, Coke will now be widely distributed through the efforts of Getranka Kombinat, an East German soft drink producer. Pepsico, with sixty-three bottling plants in Eastern Europe already, has been bartering soft drinks for vodka since 1972. More recently, it has been trading cola for Polish wooden chairs which it uses in its American Pizza Hut stores.[2]

Building Western European Market Share from Eastern Europe

General Electric Company has entered the Eastern European market in a major way by taking control of the Hungarian light bulb manufacturer, Tungsram. Its $150 million move into the Eastern Block was at least partially motivated by a frontal assault on its American light bulb market share by Philips, the international lighting leader. With only 3 percent of the European light bulb market, GE needed penetration and ready distribution.

GE saw Tungsram as its back door to the European Community. In fact, more than 50 percent of Tungsram's $300 million in pre-General Electric revenue came from Western Europe. GE's strategy involves capitalizing on Tungsram's distribution and low labor component (labor is only one-quarter of its product cost as compared to one-half in the U.S.) while it simultaneously builds knowledge of and presence in the Central European market.[3]

Guardian Industries of Northville, Michigan, is a float glass maker with two factories in Luxembourg and one in Spain. In 1988, after three years of talks and

**FIGURE 30:   WESTERN EUROPEAN FIRMS OPERATING IN
                THE EAST**

Industry	Company	Stategic Position
Machine tools, producer goods	Atlas Copco (S), Danieli (I), Deutsche Babcock (D), G. Fischer (CH), Linde (D), IWKA (D), MAN (D), Mannesmann (D), Orenstein & Koppel (D), Thyssen (D)	Well placed in Eastern Europe already; newly engaged with joint ventures
Energy supply, systems	ALSTHOM (F), ASEA/BBC (CH/S), CGE (F), Felten & Guilleaume (D), NorSk Hydro (N), RWE (D), VEBA (D)	Important suppliers of electric energy, systems, chemicals
Electric/Electronic, telecommunication	AEG (D0, ALCATEL (F), Ericsson (S), GE (UK), Siemens (D)	Well introduced in Eastern Europe
Environmental protection equipment	Bilfinger & Berger (D), GEA (D), GKN (UK), Dali & Salz (D), KSB (d), Metallgesellschaft (D), Preussage (D)	Especially geared to demand potential in E. Germany
Construction	Bouguyes (F), Dyckerhoff (D), Hochtief (D), Holderbank (CH), Holzmann (D)	Well versed in international infrastructure projects
Chemicals	BAYER (D), CIGA-GEIGY (CH), Henkel (D), HOECHST (D), Rhône-Poulenc (F), Saint Gobain (F)	Important as direct suppliers and in JV's
Automotive	Daimier Benz (D), FIAT (I), OPEL (D), Peugot (F), Volswagen (D), Volvo (S)	Direct investment in Eastern Europe
Consumer goods, retail	Horten (D), Intediscount (CH) Karstadt (D), Kaufhof (D), Massa (D), Spar (D), Salamander (D)	Initial phase of marketing launch
Medical equipment	Aesculap (D), Beiersdorf (D), Drägerwerk (D), Fresenius (D)	Suppliers for huge pent-up demand
Banks, Insurance	Allianz (D), Berliner Bank (D), Deutsche Bank (D), Dresdner Bank (D), Commerzbank (D)	Setting up shop in E. Germany

D= Germany   F=France   UK=UnitedKingdom
CH=Switzerland   Sweden   I=Italy

Source: Swiss Bank Corporation

negotiations, it purchased 80 percent of Hungarian Glassworks for $120 million. Its original intention remains unchanged: to export 50 percent of its production to Western Europe. Guardian negotiated a Hungarian central bank guarantee against expropriation and a three year grace period that allows the company to begin amortizing its loan in 1992. Hungarian law now allows the repatriation of all profits, currency conversion, the elimination of withholding tax on profits, and as with other continuing operations, a five year tax holiday. While maintaining a profitable business in its own right, Guardian will be able to take advantage of any improvements in the Central European economies.

Since early in 1989, Schwinn has had a 51 percent position in a joint venture with Csepel Works Machinery Factory and the Hungarian Institute for Energetics. Its 425 workers produce bicycles whose quality is gradually improving, although not yet enough to be marketed under the Schwinn name. Schwinn worked on its deal for well over a year and has its sights set on both the long-term Western and Eastern markets.

The New England Machinery Company (Florida) simply has included central Europe in its broader European strategy. To its Swedish R&D center and French sales office, it has added a wholly owned and low-cost Hungarian manufacturing plant.

Staking Out a Long-Term Niche in the Soviet Market

ICL (England) initiated a joint venture in 1989 with Morflot (the Soviet merchant marine) to make and sell personal computers in the U.S.S.R. ICL owns 40 percent of MCS as does Morflot. The city of Leningrad controls the remaining 20 percent, and provides space for the company's operations. The new business, Marine Computer Systems, sold 2,700 units in the U.S.S.R. in 1989.

All were shipped from the United Kingdom and assembled in Leningrad. ICL's primary partner is essential to product sale and distribution. A large part of the production that has been sold to date has been purchased by the Soviet merchant marine organization. ICL's joint venture, while profitable on a small scale, is primarily an effort to stay close to a slowly developing market that will ultimately require the kind of connections now being forged. In the meantime, the venture can take advantage of existing Russian software that, in the absence of copyright protection, can be bundled with its hardware.[4]

MicroAge Computer wanted a low-risk way into Eastern Europe and chose to take a minority position in a venture with an experienced partner. Phargo Management Corporation of Canada already had ten years of experience in the U.S.S.R. when it and MicroAge began the fifteen months of negotiations that led to the opening of a retail location in Moscow.

Those companies who have concluded deals and joint ventures in the Soviet Union have taken into account the need to deal with government bodies ranging from the Supreme Soviet to municipal governments. In arranging to explore potential oil fields, Chevron signed agreements with both the Soviet Ministry of Oil and Gas and the government of Kazakhstan. In order to open two Pizza Hut restaurants in Moscow, Pepsico signed contracts with both the Moscow city council and the borough council. It may not be clear for some time just who owns what properties in the U.S.S.R. and its provinces. Nevertheless, by early 1992, Moscow will have six western-style business hotels, Federal Express and UPS service, McDonald's, Pizza Hut and Baskin-Robbins. Hotel deals may be modeled on Marriott's 25 percent position in a joint venture with LOT (the Polish national airline) and ILBAU (an Austrian construction firm). The resulting $65 million, 520 room, 1,000 employee hotel in Warsaw employs forty American managers and charges typically Western rates.

Building a Telecommunications Infrastructure

The fact that Eastern telecommunications networks are so poorly developed presents a remarkable opportunity for cellular network designers and suppliers. The rapid development of cellular technology makes it preferable to install entire cellular systems rather than lay traditional telephone cables in these infrastructure-poor countries. In Budapest, Hungary, where it can take up to fourteen years of waiting to get a new phone line installed, U.S. West entered a joint venture with Magyas Posta (the Hungarian telecommunications and postal authority) to build the East's first cellular phone system.

Forty-nine percent owned by US West, the $26 million start-up hopes to deliver service to Budapest in 1991. US West managed to negotiate a full repatriation of its Hungarian profits and made separate arrangements for political risk insurance from the Overseas Private Investment Corporation in Washington.[5] Investment in Hungary's traditional phone system is pegged at $7 billion over the next ten years. Hungary has a joint venture with Canada's Northern Telecom and two Austrian companies to rebuild and modernize that system. The Polish government expects to spend $14 billion on a similar project. British Telecom and Swedish Telecom are joint venturing to build the Polish cellular network.

Less obvious opportunities are often easily overlooked. For example, Martech of Anchorage, Alaska, was asked by the Hungarian Ministry of Environmental Protection to clean up its military bases after the departure of Soviet troops.

Health Care Needs Cannot Wait

The telecommunications and environmental markets are just two in which pressing needs create immediate opportunity. In the healthcare field, fifty-six American companies attended the Public Health Care '90 trade show in Moscow in May of 1990. Abbott Labs, Colgate Palmolive, Hewlett Packard, Hospital Corporation of America, Pfizer, and Johnson and Johnson are just a few of those who have found health-related needs so great that Soviet buyers do not know where to look first. The Commerce Department estimates that in 1991, $950 million of medical imports will be purchased by the Soviets representing about 30 percent of their total medical purchases.

Cenogenics Corporation has capitalized on Central European medical needs by providing the Polish government with medical diagnostic kits since 1987. A Polish-born, American business broker alerted Cenogenics to the fact that the Polish government was seeking bids to provide diagnostic kits. The company's winning bid resulted in the sale of 200,000 stool blood tests. A second broker is assisting the company in establishing a joint manufacturing and distribution venture that will broaden the company's reach to the rest of Eastern Europe. The efforts of the brokers have resulted in a Polish facility for Cenogenics, funded by the state government. Cenogenics has contributed a minimal amount of capital while sending its American employees to Poland to train local personnel. Taking payment only in U.S. dollars, Cenogenics has no problem letting local companies sell its products under their own brand names.[6]

Central Europe Is Wary of Foreign Domination

After forty years of Soviet dominance, the rest of Central Europe is wary of selling out to the West. The new Hungarian government and its opposition parties have already shown concern that property valuations are unrealistically low and that Western partners and acquirers are trying to take advantage of a lack of commercial sophistication. John Kenneth Galbraith told a conference in Brussels that Central Europeans should be careful not to let foreign investors take over their industries.

The implications for Western investors are clear. Sensitivity is required. A successful business enterprise is not an end, but a means to an end. Let's be sure that in the context of the following parable we are not so clever that we destroy the mean for our long-term success.

17 A Helping Hand from the West, or Who Was That Masked Man?

On a collective farm on the outskirts of Prague, Czechoslovakia, a meeting was held in the wake of the sudden political and economic emancipation of Eastern Europe. A pig sat comfortably in large pool of mud, while a chicken paraded her chicks nearby. The chicken gradually made her way over to the pig and began a conversation.

"You know," she said, "without state control of production, supply, and pricing, a tremendous pent-up demand for food is about to be unleashed."

"So?" responded the nonplused pig.

"So, now is our chance to start a profitable business of our own, to be our own bosses, and to work our own hours!"

"You're beginning to make some sense. What do you suggest?" asked the pig.

"I suggest that we start a joint venture," answered the hen.

"What is a joint venture?" queried the pig, a blank look on his face.

The hen responded, "A joint venture means that we will pool our resources and expertise, work together, and produce something that people want so badly that we will make a tidy profit selling it."

The pig looked confused. "What is a profit?" he asked.

Exasperated, the hen replied, "Profit is the money that will be left over after we make and sell the new product. We can use that money any way we want—to make your slop hole bigger, for example."

The pig was clearly impressed. "That sounds great. What product should we make."

The hen thought for a moment before speaking, being careful to choose just the right words. "I know," she said, "ham and eggs!"

The pig recoiled. "That hardly seems fair. You are asking me to contribute my life while you go about your everyday business of producing eggs."

"Well, maybe," said the hen, "but with my business and management expertise we can give you a slop hole twice the size of the one you have now!"

DIRECTORY OF EUROPEAN INFORMATION SOURCES

18

Directory of European Information Sources

Tere is a variety of public and private organizations which have compiled and published information on the European Community and its Single Market Plan. Much of this is issued in the form of reports and newsletters on various industry, trade, or political topics germane to an organization's areas of concern.

The listing that follows can be used as a source for direct contact with individuals with whom you can talk in order to solicit answers to specific questions, or as a source for a continuous flow of reports and updates on your areas of market interest. Many of the publications produced by the organizations listed here are available at little or no cost.

Official Sources of Information on the European Community

1. *The European Community Information Service*, Delegation of the Commission of the European Community, 305 E. 47th Street, New York, NY 10017; phone: (212) 371-3804
   2100 M Street, N.W., Washington, DC 20037; phone: (202) 862-9500

2. *Office of European Community Affairs*, Single Market Information Service, U.S. Department of Commerce, Room 3036, 14th & Constitution Avenue, N.W., Washington, DC 20230

3. *The Council of Ministers of the European Community*, 170 rue de la Loi, Brussels, B-10048, Belgium; phone: 32-2-235-61-11

4. *The European Commission*, 200 rue de la Loi, Brussels, B-1040, Belgium; phone: 32-2-235-11-11

5. *The European Parliament*, 97 rue Belliard, Brussels, B-1040, Belgium; phone: 32-2-234-21-11

6. *The European Court of Justice*, Centre European, Plateau de Kirschberg, Luxembourg; phone: 43-67-66

7. *U.S. Mission to the European Community*, Boulevard du Regent 40, Brussels, Belgium; phone: 32-2-513-3830

8. *American Chamber of Commerce in Belgium*, EC Affairs Office, Avenue des Arts 50, Bte. 5, B-1040, Brussels, Belgium

9. *Office of European Commission Affairs*, International Trade Administration, U.S. Department of Commerce, Washington, DC 20230; phone: (202) 377-5279

10. *Office for Europe & the Mediterranean*, Office of the U.S. Trade Representative, 600 17th Street, N.W., Washington, DC 20506; phone: (202) 395-4620

11. *Office of Developed Country Trade*, Bureau of Economic and Business Affairs, U.S. Department of State, Washington, DC 20520; phone: (202) 647-1162

For financial information

12. *International Finance Division*, Federal Reserve System, 20th Street & Constitution Avenue, N.W., Washington, DC 20551; phone: (202) 452-3614

For information on the specification of product standards

13. *American National Standards Institute*, 1430 Broadway, New York, NY 10018; phone: (212) 354-3300 (also has a branch at the American Chamber of Commerce in Brussels; see # 8 above)

14. *National Bureau of Standards*, Administration Building, Room A629, Gaithersburg, MD 20899; phone: (301) 974-4040

15. *CEN/CENELEC*, 2 rue Brederode, Bte. 5, 1000 Brussels, Belgium; phone: 519-6811

For political & trade concerns in the telecommunications industry

16. *Bureau of International Communications and Information Policy*, U.S. Department of State, Washington, DC 20520; phone: (202) 647-5727

17. Office of International Affairs, National Telecommunications and Information Administration, U.S. Department of Commerce, Washington, DC 20230; phone: (202) 377-1304

For EC member state overview and opinion

18. *Confederation of British Industry*, Centre Point, 103 New Oxford Street, London, WC1A 1DU, United Kingdom

19. *Conseil National du Patronat Francais*, 31 Avenue Pierre ler de Serbie, 75116 Paris, France

20. *German Industry Federation*, Gustav-Heinemann-Ufer 84-88, Postfach 51-05-48, D-5000 Koeln 51 (Bayenthal), Germany
    also: One Farragut Square South, 1634 Eye Street, N.W., Washington, DC 20006

21. *UNICE*, Rue Joseph II, 40-Bte.4, 1040 Brussels, Belgium

For both overview and specific industry information, the following trade associations can be of assistance.

22. *National Association of Manufacturers*, 1331 Pennsylvania Avenue, N.W., Suite 1500, Washington, DC 20004-1703; phone: (202) 637-3000

23. *Semiconductor Industry Association*, 10201 Torre Avenue, Suite 275, Cupertino, CA 95014; phone: (408) 973-0289

24. *Air Transport Association of America*, 1709 New York Avenue, N.W., Washington, DC 20006; phone: (202) 626-4000

25. *American Trucking Associations*, 2200 Mill Road, Alexandria, VA 22314; phone: (703) 838-1700

26. *National Solid Waste Management Association*, 1730 Rhode Island Avenue, N.W., Suite 1000, Washington, DC 20036; phone: (202) 659-4613

27. *Air Conditioning & Refrigeration Institute*, 1501 Wilson Boulevard, Suite 600, Arlington, VA 22209-2403; phone: (703) 524-8800

28. *Pharmaceutical Manufacturers Association*, 1100 15th Street, N.W., Suite 900, Washington, DC 20005; phone: (202) 835-3400

29. *Material Handling Institute*, 8720 Red Oak Boulevard, Suite 201, Charlotte, NC 28217

30. *Aerospace Industries Association of America*, 1250 Eye Street, N.W., Suite 1100, Washington, DC; phone: (202) 371-8400

31. *Security Industry Association*, 2800 28th Street, Suite 101, Santa Monica, CA 90405; phone: (213) 450-4141

32. *Semiconductor Equipment & Materials International*, 805 E. Middlefield Road, Mountain View, CA 94043, phone: (415) 964-5111

33. *Rubber Manufacturers Association*, 1400 K Street, N.W., Washington, DC 20005; phone: (202) 682-4800

34. *International Franchise Association*, 1350 New York Avenue, N.W., Suite 900, Washington, DC 20005; phone: (202) 628-8000

35. *American Paper Institute*, 260 Madison Avenue, 10th Floor, New York, NY 10016; phone: (212) 340-0600

36. *Computer and Communication Industry Association*, 666 11th Street, N.W., Washington, DC 20001; phone: (202) 783-0070

37. *Computer & Business Equipment Manufacturers Association*, 311 First Street, N.W., Suite 500, Washington, DC 20001; phone: (202) 737-8888

For trade promotion information from eleven of the twelve EC member states:

38. *European-American Chambers of Commerce*, 666 Fifth Avenue, New York, NY 10103; phone: (212) 974-8843

For information on the rules, regulations, and conduct of international trade and negotiations:

39. *GATT Secretariate*, 154 rue de Lausanne, 1211 Geneva 21, Switzerland

For information on product quality standards:

40. *CECC General Secretariat*, Stressemannallee 15, D-6000 Frankfurt/M70, Germany; phone: 49-69-630-8283

41. *International Electrotechnical Commission Central Office*, 3 rue de Varembe, 1211 Geneva 20, Switzerland; phone: 41-22-734-0150

42. *British Quality Standards*, BSI, Linfordwood, Milton Keynes, England, United Kingdom MK14 6LE; phone: 44-908-22-11-66

43. *Electronic Components Certification Board*, Electronics Industry Association, 2001 I Street, N.W., Washington, DC 20006; phone: (202) 245-4961

To get a start on Central and Eastern Europe

44. *U.S. Department of Commerce, International Trade Administration*, East Europe Information Center; phone: (202) 377-2645

45. *U.S. Department of Commerce, International Trade Administration, Support for Eastern European Democracy (SEED)*; phone: (202) 377-2645

46. *US Chamber of Commerce, Central and Eastern European Trade and Technical Assistance Center;* phone: (202) 463-5482

To find a translator

47. *U.S. Department of State*; phone: (202) 634-3600

To find agents and connections to trade in the East

48. *The Directory of Foreign Trade Organizations in Eastern Europe*, International Trade Press, 2 Townsend Street, #2-304 San Francisco, CA 94107; phone: (415) 495-4765 (contains 3,000 listings of organizations which are active in foreign trade and related activities including chambers of commerce, ministries, agents).

APPENDIX

"EUROPSEAK" GLOSSARY OF THE NEW EUROPE

19 EUROSPEAK: The Language of the New Europe

A merica is an economic, Darwinian petrie dish—a sort of controlled experiment in the context of which varied enterprises, playing by a single set of fixed rules, battle for survival and growth. Its expensive and liberated market place is about as close as the world has been able to come to a fiscal Utopia.

This unique, open economy, in which people and capital move as they please, provides economies of a scale that allow investments in development to be spread over fifty states and two hundred and fifty million consumers.

This is the model and measuring stick for the New Europe—a collection of sometimes totalitarian and at other times democratic nation-states, with often interdependent feudal and monarchic histories. As a group of unrelated cultures, governments, and economies, Europe simply could not justify the costs of innovation in divided markets across which development costs could never be amortized.

225

The nearly thirty years of stubborn European resistance to a market union has been a source of continuing benefit to the United States. The result of the post-World War II rebuilding of Western Europe was the creation of a host of new and independent markets for American manufacturers and marketers. Subsequent to developing products and services in domestic markets, American firms could enter new foreign markets with often agreeable Western tastes and pricing. Separated by culture and language as much as by border restrictions, European competition offered little resistance to market-tested American products. Marketing skills were often secondary to the force and staying power of the offer. What's more, American and later Japanese, companies were developing international business expertise at the expense of European competitors who could rarely justify venturing beyond their own borders.

Side stepping its pledge to create a pan-European economic market, Europe instead began assembling a piecemeal defense composed of artificial trade barriers—a defense that locked industry into a cycle of decreasing global efficiency and competitiveness. After years of minimal growth, Europeans faced some clear choices: second-class status in the context of a declining standard of living or economic revival based on the sacrifice of national economic sovereignty.

A new drive toward unity, based on the "four freedoms," so ably exploited by Americans, then began. Barriers to the free movement of people, capital, goods, and services were systematically removed. A new European union was being incubated, with delivery scheduled for December 31, 1992.

Like all institutions, the New Europe has developed its own language. Worse still, the acronyms that comprise this new "Eurospeak" augment an already confusing array of international trade terminology.

An American company getting its first exposure to European trade, or one newly cognizant of the legal and market trends affecting its industry, will be confronted and confounded by jumbles of words like these:

The Uruguay Round of GATT has pushed the EC, with advice from EFTA, to consider the issue of CEPT objection to the addition of ETSI to the excluded sectors framework, whether or not VAT's are harmonized or VRA's dropped.

HELP!!!

What follows, then, is a brief primer on "Eurospeak." While the language grows daily, the following glossary is a start toward an understanding of the players and the ground rules in the EC today.

EUROSPEAK GLOSSARY:
The Language of the New Europe

I. THE INSTITUTIONS

EC (The European Community) or the EEC
(The European Economic Community)

The EC is a political and economic alliance of twelve Western European countries that was initiated in 1957 with the Treaty of Rome. Known popularly for many years as the European Common Market, its original member countries were France, Belgium, West Germany, Italy, Luxembourg, and the Netherlands. A customs union was achieved in 1968 which eliminated intra-EC tariffs while arranging for common external tariffs. Denmark, the United Kingdom, Greece, Spain, Ireland and Portugal have subsequently been accepted as members. In the late 1980s a plan for the removal of all non-tariff barriers by the end of 1992 was implemented. The term European Economic Community has fallen into disuse because of the broader political and social aspirations of the agents of change in Europe.

Jacques Delors and others with pan-European visions see the EC as a kind of European confederation whose federal policy supersedes that of its individual states.

In addition to the free movement of goods, services, people, and capital, single monetary and social policies are sought for the entire continent.

EFTA (European Free Trade Association)

Established in 1960 by Austria, Denmark, Norway, Portugal, Sweden, Switzerland, and the United Kingdom, EFTA's goal was to liberalize trade. As the EC has rushed toward the completion of the Single Market, EFTA has progressed from something of a poor man's EC to a sister organization which is likely to share in all trade liberalization instituted by the EC. Finland and Iceland joined in 1961 and 1970 respectively. By 1966 most of the tariff barriers between the EFTA countries had been eliminated. Denmark and the U.K. left to join the EC in 1973, as did Portugal in 1986.

While EFTA has in some respects become a kind of "taxi squad" for EC membership, it serves a particularly important function for neutral countries such as Switzerland, who for historic and political reasons must tiptoe very carefully around membership in any club that implies political affiliation. The economic integration of EFTA and its thirty-two million citizens with the EC is being accomplished at the moment without the monetary, social, and political ramifications of EC membership feared by Switzerland, Sweden, and Finland. The European Economic Space (see below) promises to extend the economic and trade policies of the EC to EFTA as well.

EES (European Economic Space)

What do you call the common territory occupied by two clubs that want to cooperate, but who have not only different members but different rules? The EES defines a "space" in which all trade barriers—both tariff and non-tariff in nature—will be cleared. In addition, the two organizations will cooperate on research and development programs. The practical reasons for finding an umbrella under which both the EC and EFTA can play are overwhelming. Trade between the two was over $220 billion in 1988 as compared to $164 billion between the U.S. and the EC. This eighteen country free trade zone is quite likely to grow over time, as the EC reviews new membership applications and as expansion pressure builds from both Western and Central Europe.

The European Commission

The European Commission is one of the four branches of EC government. It is something of an amalgam of both the executive and legislative branches of the U.S. government. Seventeen commissioners comprise the body: two each from France, Germany, Italy, Spain, and the United Kingdom, and one each from the other member states. The commissioners are appointed by their national governments and are responsible as a group for the initiation, formulation, and submission of EC legislation. Once appointed, the commissioners represent EC interests and not those of their home governments. Each commissioner oversees a specific area of responsibility on a Community-wide basis. The European Commission, located in Brussels, employs a staff of over 10,000.

The European Council of Ministers

This group of political representatives from each of the twelve member countries is the decision making body of the EC. The ministers represent the interests of their individual countries when debating and deciding (most often by a simple majority) the approval of legislation brought to them by the European Commission. The resulting directives and regulations must be implemented by the member states within a predetermined period of time. Germany, the U.K., France, and Italy each have ten representatives. Spain has eight, and Belgium, Greece, the Netherlands, and Portugal five each. Denmark and Ireland have three members and Luxembourg has two. While there are monthly ministerial meetings, there are major gatherings twice a year.

The European Parliament

The members of this body are the only directly elected representatives of European citizenry. Elected every five years, the powers of the members are considerably less than those of parliaments who represent countries having longer histories of representative rule. The three primary tasks of the Parliament are to debate and alter legislation passed by the Council, review, and reject (if necessary) the EC budget and to dismiss the Commission (never used). Its more than 500 elected representatives act as Europeans rather than Frenchmen, for example, and are grouped according to nine political party affiliations (the Socialist Party, the European People's Party, the Green Party, etc.). By American standards, the electoral process is a lot closer to a public opinion poll than to a congressional election (Figure 31).

European Court of Justice

Unlike the United States Supreme Court, the Court of Justice is composed of thirteen judges and six advocate-generals, appointed for six year terms at the agreement of the twelve member governments. While the Court has ruled on a variety of weighty matters—including mutual recognition, merger and competition policy and trade barriers—it has become extremely overworked and has very limited compliance powers.

Some of the more notable results of cases decided by the Court include forcing Germany to open its domestic market to the import of a French alcoholic bev-

FIGURE 31:   THE EUROPEAN PARLIAMENT: POLITICAL MAKEUP BEFORE THE 1989 ELECTION

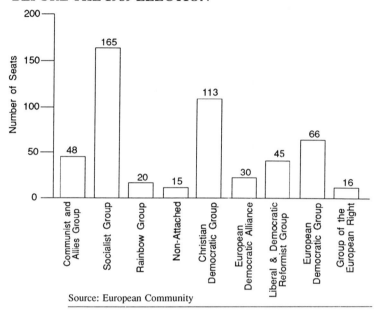

Source: European Community

erage that did not meet restrictive German alcoholic content requirements; the imposition of sanctions on a cartel of pulp and paper companies who engaged in price fixing within the Community; and striking down German "purity laws" that restricted the import of beer.

UNICE (EC-wide Employers Association)

This federation of European trade associations is lobbying and advising the EC. It has its headquarters in Brussels.

EEA (European Environmental Agency)

The EEA was created by the EC to be little more than a clearinghouse for environmental data and information, with a monitoring function thrown in. Funding from the

Community for environmental clean-up and investment is being provided separately, and suggestions of an American-style "superfund" are being pursued.

By 1993, however, the Council of Ministers will give new thought to the role of the EEA, with an eye toward endowing it with regulatory powers. Membership in the EEA will not be limited to the EC member states but is likely to include other Central European nations and possibly North African nations as well.

While the public level of European environmental concern has generally been several years behind that of the U.S., the rapid consolidation of the EC and concerns about heavily polluted Eastern European countries are resulting in EC adherence to the highest common enforcement standards where ever possible. Citizens of EC member states will have access to any official environmental information beginning in 1993. Member states are drawing up waste management plans and are issuing disposal permits. Liability for waste problems will be in the hands of producers, holders and disposers of waste. Companies are being required to dispose of waste as near to the production site as possible without transporting the waste internationally.

CEPT (European Confederation of Postal and Telecommunications Administrations)

State-controlled European communications agencies are called PTT's (postal, telephone and telegraph). While these have been gradually deregulated, all public communications networks were, until recently, controlled by separate national monopolies. CEPT, a twenty-six nation conference of national PTT's, had controlled the technical standard setting process throughout Europe for many years. Now, with the opening of these formerly restricted national markets, the EC has established ETSI (European Telecommunications Standards Institute) to give network operators, equipment manufacturers, users, and research and development organizations a chance to become a part of a process that may well determine the viability of new equipment and the direction of technological development. Non-EC standards and manufacturing bodies have been allowed a limited observer's role in order to be able to monitor technical progress.

EOTC (European Organization for Testing and Certification)

Set up by the European Commission in cooperation with EFTA and the primary EC standards groups, CEN/CENELEC (see below), EOTC addresses issues of conformity assessment, mutual confidence among test houses, and mutual recognition of test certificates in non-regulated sectors. It is charged with establishing a set of criteria for private, bilateral agreements between EC/EFTA and U.S. test houses.

STANDARDS

The issue of EC technical standards is being addressed by the Community in order to consolidate and harmonize the standards setting process. In 1990, more than 100,000 industrial standards and technical regulations applied to various business activities in the EC. For example, the European electronics industry has been covered by two sets of quality standards. ISO-9000 is the world-wide standard for quality management systems and governs the manufacturing quality of all products. CECC (Electronic Components Committee of CENELEC) has created a standard that is accepted by fifteen European countries. In addition, BS-9000 (the British standard) and IECQ (the International Electrotechnical Commission Quality system) cover specifications, approval, and the distribution of electronic components. While the intent is to do so, no one can be absolutely sure just when CECC will be phased into a new "harmonized" standards body, and if its regime will be accepted. In any case, standards issues get progressively more important, particularly in light of the new industrial emphasis on quality, the Baldridge Award in the U.S., and its new counterpart in Europe, EFQM (European Foundation for Quality Management).

FIGURE 32:   PRODUCT STANDARDS & REGULATIONS AFFECTING A TYPICAL "PAN- EUROPEAN" PRODUCT

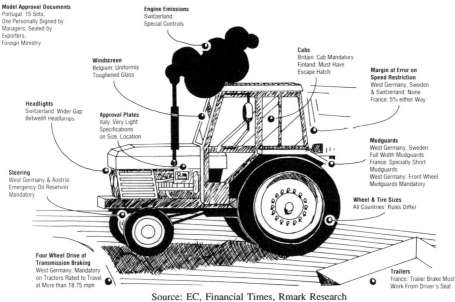

Model Approval Documents
Portugal: 15 Sets,
One Personally Signed by
Managers, Sealed by
Exporters,
Foreign Ministry

Engine Emissions
Switzerland:
Special Controls

Cabs
Britain: Cab Mandatory
Finland: Must Have
Escape Hatch

**Margin of Error on
Speed Restriction**
West Germany, Sweden
& Switzerland: None
France: 5% either Way

Windscreen
Belgium: Uniformly
Toughened Glass

Headlights
Switzerland: Wider Gap
Between Headlamps

Approval Plates
Italy: Very Light
Specifications
on Size, Location

Mudguards
West Germany, Sweden:
Full Width Mudguards
France: Specially Short
Mudguards
West Germany: Front Wheel
Mudguards Mandatory

Steering
West Germany & Austria:
Emergency Oil Reservoir
Mandatory

Wheel & Tire Sizes
All Countries' Rules Differ

**Four Wheel Drive of
Transmission Braking**
West Germany: Mandatory
on Tractors Rated to Travel
at More than 18.75 mph

Trailers
France: Trailer Brake Must
Work From Driver's Seat

Source: EC, Financial Times, Rmark Research

There are a number of national standards bodies within the EC whose functions will ultimately be eclipsed and absorbed by the broadly accepted EC bodies:

DIN/BSI/AFNOR

These national standards setting bodies (Germany, Britain, and France respectively) will disappear into

CEN/CENELEC. There is some resentment within the EC over the fact that Germans seem to have a disproportionately large say in standards issues since they chair two out of every five standards-setting committees under the CEN/CENELEC umbrella.

CEN (European Committee for Standards

CENELEC (European Committee for Electrotechnical Standardization)

ISO (International Standards Organization)

IEC (International Electrotechnical Commission

ISO and IEC are international organizations with ample American representation. The EC has promised to coordinate its own standards setting activities with those of the international organizations, at least partly to relieve itself of added and unnecessarily redundant responsibility.

ETSI (European Telecommunications Standards Institute)

In conjunction with CEN/CENELEC, ETSI will establish European standards for telecommunications equipment and services. It removes this function from the exclusive control of CEPT, which includes only PTT's as members. ETSI includes the PTT's, equipment and service providers, and user groups as well.

IEPG (Independent European Program Group)

Founded in 1986, the IEPG aims to increase common defense procurement in Europe, as well as military staff interaction among thirteen European countries. This area is beyond the purview of Community trade rules as it is specifically excluded by the Treaty of Rome. As a practical matter, U.S. companies and Europeans alike are facing competition for a piece of a progressively smaller defense pie. European defense companies are going through a wave of consolidation as well. General Electric Company (UK) took over Ferranti. Daimler-Benz took over MBB and Deutche Aerospace. And Matra (France) acquired Fairchild Aircraft.

ETUC (European Trade Union Confederation)

ETUC represents 44 million workers from twenty-one Western European countries. It manages to get its voice heard in the review of nearly all pieces of EC legislation.

BEUC (European Bureau of Consumers Unions)

A combination of twenty consumers unions from the twelve EC member states, BEUC is a major source of information for the European Parliament.

EEB (European Environmental Bureau)

This lobbying group shares its concern for the environment with the Institute for European Policy on Environment, both of whom seek a hearing in Brussels.

II. INSTITUTIONAL LANGUAGE

Directives

A directive is a piece of EC legislation, drafted by the European Commission, reviewed by the European Parliament and adopted by the European Council of Ministers. Binding on each member state, the directive must be implemented within two years in conjunction with each nation's own regulations and laws.

Regulations

Originated and approved in much the same way as directives, regulations contain details essential to the implementation of existing legislation. Regulations become EC law as soon as they are adopted by the European Council of Ministers.

The White Paper

Titled, "Completing the Internal Market," the White Paper, as it became known, was a special study directed by Lord Cockfield, former EC Commissioner for Internal Market Affairs. This discussion paper listed nearly 300 proposed directives which the author believed to be essential for the achievement of a true "common market." The White Paper included a timetable which detailed the dismantling of all physical and technical barriers within the European Community by December 31, 1992.

Green Paper

Prepared by the European Commission, this is the generic EC name for a "red herring." This trial balloon is something of a first draft of legislation, usually describing multiple policy options in a particular industry or other area of interest. The green paper of June 30, 1987, on telecommunications created a stir of controversy both within and beyond the Community. It proposed a compromise between the traditional public ownership of basic telecommunication network services and the more recent trend toward free markets in services using networks and equipment that can be linked. While this position would allow the PTT's to participate in competitive services, reserved services (basic phone access) would be the domain of the PTT's alone. Competitive services would include value-added services and intelligent networks, for example.

The Cecchini Report

Commissioned by the EC and compiled by Paolo Cecchini, this report was officially titled, "The European Challenge, 1992." Delivered in 1988 to the Commissioner for the Single Internal Market, the report gave a prognosis for a united Europe. The report took as a given that the directives in the 1985 White Paper would be fully implemented by the end of 1992. Cecchini used his report to trace the failure of the EC to achieve its long-stated goal of unification. In doing so, he specified the cost of that failure in quantitative terms. A prognosis for development of the Single Market after 1992 was also provided.

Cecchini concluded that full implementation of the White Paper would result in GDP growth in the Community of between 4.5 and 7 percent; a price level reduction of between 4.5 and 6 percent; the creation of 1.8 million new jobs; and an improvement in the external balance of trade of 1 percent. The psychology of expansion would result in a supply-side led recovery. Its assumptions about complete and timely conformance by the member states has been unreasonably optimistic, as changes in border controls, public procurement, and financial markets have come more slowly than hoped. Business will also have to adapt to significant structural change. While frequently criticized, the report provided the spark needed to keep EC momentum building.

SEA (Single European Act)

This amendment to the Treaty of Rome, effective in July 1987, specified several changes designed to hasten the completion of the Single Market:

• completion of the European internal market by the end of 1992,

• improvement in regional research and technological development,

- movement toward a European economic and monetary union,

- improvement of environmental and working conditions, and

- qualified majority voting, rather than unanimity, in most cases, in order to keep EC regulation from being blocked.

The SEA specified the evolution of a single market, without internal frontiers, and guaranteed the free movement of people, goods, services, and capital within those frontiers.

IGC (Intergovernmental Conference)

In roughly the same way that the U.S. government can use a constitutional convention, the EC can use the IGC. Such a conference has been called to pressure the twelve members to close in on solutions to eventual monetary and political union.

Association Agreements

Akin to economic treaties, Association Agreements have already been concluded with Cyprus, Malta, and Turkey in order to bring these countries closer to the more open, EC model. It is assumed that the non-EC countries with whom such agreements are written will eventually become applicants to join the EC. The Turkish agreement actually offers membership.

Second Generation Agreements

Association Agreements between the EC and the former Eastern Block countries go beyond previous treaties and agreements in that they provide for free-trade arrangements, cultural and political relationships, and financial aid.

Community "Deepening" or "Widening"

What makes for a stronger club—a solid core, or wider membership? This question is at the heart of a continuing EC debate, highlighted by the sudden dismemberment of the Eastern Block. The French are strongly in favor of completion of the Single Market in all of its detail, including its political, social, and monetary aspects, before widening its membership. The U.K., on the other hand, believes that membership should quickly be extended to the surrounding countries including EFTA and the Central European states.

III. THE LANGUAGE OF INTERNATIONAL TRADE

GATT (General Agreement on Tariffs and Trade)

Nearly 100 countries belong to this group, created in 1948 to promote a code of fair trade practices among its members. The group has periodic rounds of trade negotiations, each focusing on specific issues or problems. The Kennedy Round of negotiations (from 1964–67) took a product-by-product approach in order to reduce tariffs. The Tokyo Round (1973–79) concentrated on additional tariff cuts and also developed a series of agreements on non-tariff measures. The Uruguay Round (1986–90) was aimed at strengthening GATT and expanding its coverage to other areas, including subsidization of agriculture, local content rules (see below), quantitative restrictions, import licenses, and other barriers to market entry.

Policy on each of these issues varies from EC member to member, with Spain, for example, having eliminated all of its QR's and licensing restrictions with the U.S. upon its entry into the EC in 1986. The concerns for open markets for various services are being considered within this framework at the GNS (Group Negotiations on Services).

The Uruguay Round, so named because its first meeting was held in Punta del Este, Uruguay, was to be completed by the end of 1990. Pitted against one another were the developing countries of Latin America and Asia and the developed, industrialized nations. The developing nations demanded fair markets for their labor intensive agricultural and textile industries. The developed nations insisted on winning freedom for their service industries (financial, construction, etc.) to operate anywhere.

FIGURE 33:   EXAMPLES OF QUANTITATIVE RESTRICTIONS (QA'S) IN THE EC IN 1988

Product	# of EC-Wide Restrictions	Additional Member State Restrictions
Steel	14	United Kingdom
Agriculture and Food Products	36	France, Ireland, Italy
Automobiles and Transport Equipment	2	France, Italy, Portugal, Spain, United Kingdom
Textiles and Clothing	18	Germany, United Kingdom
Electronic Products	5	France, Italy, United Kingdom
Footwear	1	France, Italy, United Kindom
Machine Tools	2	United Kingdom

Source: GATT, "Review of Developments in The Trading System," 1988

Simultaneously, they demanded protection for their intellectual property (through uniformly recognized copyright and patent protection).

European agricultural subsidies were a major stumbling block. There are ten million farmers in the EC (as compared to the two and one-half million in the U.S.) and the EC guarantees the local market of each while underwriting his exports with a $10 billion annual fund. Germany, in particular, has institutionalized farm inefficiency by encouraging subsidized farming as a second income source for the typical southern German factory worker.

Developing countries are fighting to get the U.S. to drop its protection of the textile and apparel industries—and their arguments are strong ones. William Cline, a senior fellow at the Institute for International Economics in Washington, DC, was quoted in *Fortune Magazine* (8/27/90, p.77) as having calculated that protectionism typically added 50 percent to wholesale clothing costs in the U.S.

In the services sector, some countries have laughably restrictive laws, Turkey forbids international accounting firms from using outside capital to set up offices, and requires them to take a local partner and use only its name in any promotional activities. In the area of intellectual property, most developing countries have no laws at all. It is estimated that American companies lose more than $30 billion per year through the theft of intellectual property. *Fortune Magazine* notes that Pfizer invests an average of $230 million and ten years in the development of a new drug, a process that can be duplicated by a clever third-world chemist in a matter of weeks.

OECD (Organization of Economic Cooperation and Development)

In working with the United Nations and the International Monetary Fund, this group of industrialized countries aims to make foreign trade data as compatible and useful as possible. The organization promotes economic cooperation and publishes a great deal of information on economic and trade topics.

Harmonized Schedule

Tariff nomenclature classifies traded goods on a six-digit code basis. National distinctions are introduced for tariff or statistical purposes beyond the six-digit level. The European countries accepted this standard in 1988. The Tariff Schedule of the U.S. was replaced by this code in 1989.

BTN (Brussels Tariff Nomenclature)

This commodity classification system was used until recently by most major international trading companies. It categorized products for tariff and statistical purposes and has now been replaced by CCCN (Customs Cooperation Council Nomenclature).

Reciprocity

Before foreign business organizations can locate and begin operating in Europe, European companies must be able to establish themselves in that non-EC country. This principle, introduced by the EC in all of its trade policy negotiations with outsiders, is a sticking point in specific industries, and to a greater degree with Japan and other Asian countries than with the U.S. A non-EC company can expect access to the EC marketplace in its industry only to the extent that its home country extends operating rights to EC firms wishing to do business there.

In the Uruguay Round of GATT negotiations, for example, the EC demanded that the U.S. force its telecommunications companies (the Baby Bells) to open bidding on equipment contracts to European suppliers on the same basis as such European bidding is desirable for U.S. suppliers. While American negotiators reply that private U.S. telcom companies are not under government control, there are a variety of American programs in place which discourage foreign sourcing. As a consequence, American telecom companies are faced with a local content rule in European contract sourcing that will often preclude U.S. companies from a clean shot at European PTT business. Allowing you to have the same opportunity in my market as I have in yours is called *Comparable Access*.

National Treatment

In 1976, all members of the OECD (including the U.S. and the EC member states) signed a non-binding National Treatment Instrument. This doctrine of international law requires that foreign enterprises be treated on the same basis as domestic enterprises in the market place: we treat *your* companies in *our markets* in the same way that we treat our own companies in those markets. The Treaty of Rome also requires that no such distinctions be made. Yet EC draft directives have given foreign companies cause for worry.

Domestic Origin (Local Content)

This non-tariff, political, and economic definition of a product's origin is an effective protectionist barrier to the import of goods whose component value and labor content comes largely from abroad. If the local content of a product is less than 45 percent (rule-of-thumb) of the value of that product, various duties will be attached to the price of that product upon import. The higher price generally excludes the imported product from competing effectively in the local market. In the U.S. such rules have been proposed to penalize automobiles, which, while assembled in the U.S., are built largely from foreign components.

In the late 1980s, the EC determined that Ricoh copier machines being imported from a plant in California were built from Japanese parts whose assembly in the U.S. did not qualify them as U.S. manufactured products. Duties were levied that were comparable to those of any other product imported from Japan. While this rule has not been applied and this early decision was reversed, the case has given notice to those who would hope to build "screwdriver"-type assembly plants in order to qualify for national treatment (see above).

Directives for the four excluded sectors (see below) specify that the value of the EC content of a contract bid must be more than 50 percent or the bid may either be removed from consideration, or penalized with a 3 percent compensating price adjustment. In the broadcast sector, an EC directive requires that broadcasters seek to fill at least half of their broadcast time with programming produced in the EC. While the purpose of such laws is to protect local industry as it develops its talent and quality, the effect is actually to create an inefficient, non-competitive, protected local industry—albeit one that is guaranteed survival for the short-term.

The long-term inability of the protected market to adjust to global, structural, and technological changes insures a competitive disadvantage against those who must survive or perish in a comparatively free market.

MTN (Multi-lateral Trade Negotiations)

This is nothing more than the shorthand for the GATT trade negotiations which are held periodically for the purpose of maximizing the growth of world trade through the reduction of tariff and non-tariff barriers.

Parallel Trade

The ability to buy products in one market where they are relatively inexpensive and to then sell them in other markets where they are more expensive is the essence of parallel trade. The effect of such practices is often supply dislocation, artificially induced shortages, or oversupplies. While the EC is gradually eliminating such practices with the opening of borders and the harmonizing of pricing, parallel trade has served a very useful purpose in the past. The effect of its supply and demand "arbitrage" has helped to moderate price fluctuations and inflationary pressure.

COCOM (Coordinating Committee on Multi-Lateral Export Controls)

This informal international export-control organization exists primarily as a forum for the industrial democracies to get together and discuss unilateral export restrictions. Of greatest concern are sensitive, high-technology products that may have national security implications. Cocom keeps a list of goods that need special licenses to be shipped to Eastern Europe or to China. The U.S. has worked out agreements with individual EC countries concerning the re-export of some of these sensitive products. However, at some point, this arrangement will have to be renegotiated under EC authority rather than that of individual member states (all EC countries, with the exception of Ireland, are members of Cocom).

Upward Harmonization

The process of harmonizing many varied policies and product standards to the highest common denominator is what seems to be taking place within the EC. This implies that those states currently paying the most attention to safety and environmental concerns, for example, will have standards similar to their own adopted by the EC. It would be wise, therefore, for an American pollution control equipment maker to study the German environmental control equipment standards before bidding on EC contracts in this field.

Bi-Lateral Recognition Agreements

These are agreements between the EC and third-party, non-EC trading partners concerning the testing and certification of products that will be exported to the European Community. The EC will negotiate these agreements (which for logistic purposes are essential for U.S. exporters) on the following conditions:

- the EC must be assured of the technical competence of the non-EC partner,

- the agreement specifies reciprocal benefits, and

- only testing and certification bodies can actually participate in the agreements.

Substantial Transformation

This term is a test of local content, used in the U.S. for example, to determine the country in which the most recent substantial process or operation was economically justified and performed. The EC also uses this terminology and has adopted specific criteria for televisions, tape recorders, textiles, ceramics, roller bearings, and other products. Based on this term, a winning argument was made for a 1989 directive which will force many semiconductor manufacturers to divert production from the U.S. or far East to Europe. That directive specifies semiconductor wafer fabrication as the last substantial product transformation. U.S. and Japanese semiconductor manufacturers who want to ensure that their products will retain major market positions are being forced to consider building manufacturing facilities in the EC.

Forced Investment

Local content rules, whose intent is to exclude products of foreign origin, place exporters at a competitive disadvantage. The only way for the foreign manufacturer to overcome this disadvantage is through a direct investment in a European facility or in a European joint venture. Both Intel and Fujitsu have been forced into this position in the semiconductor business in order to protect market share. While this may have positive employment effects in the EC country of choice, it may still allow foreign dominance of a particular industry.

Separately, such large investments ($400 million by Intel, $600 million by Fujitsu) shift jobs and technological development abroad at the expense of the U.S. and Japanese economies.

Dumping

This protectionist euphemism has applications in the EC comparable to those in the U.S. When an industry is threatened by lower cost imported competition, it routinely seeks help from the domestic trade authorities who, after examining the situation, may determine that the imports are being priced below their reasonable cost. This subsidization of exports is considered to be dumping by the nation of import, and duties are imposed on the imported products to level the playing field.

VRA (Voluntary Restraint Agreement)

VRA's have been used in the automotive and certain other industries in the EC in order to put a "voluntary" quota on the numbers of cars, for example, that can be imported from a given country over a twelve month period. While the objective of the VRA is to temporarily prevent domination of a home market by foreign competition, the restrictions are not necessarily temporary, nor do they help guarantee improvements in the home industry. Without VRA's, the German auto market has managed to hold off the Japanese, while with VRA's the U.S. auto market is increasingly vulnerable. Ultimately, the EC will eliminate individual national VRA's in favor of Community-wide VRA's to be negotiated from Brussels.

Substitution Effect

All things being otherwise equal, buyers will generally favor local suppliers over distant ones who may have problematic delivery or service. In the absence of inter-European border restrictions, a substitution of local products from within neighboring member states for those that are imported from distant trading partners is likely—if they are comparable in quality and cost. For example, there is likely to be an increase in the use of Scandinavian and French products within Germany, to the detriment of American products which had previously occupied that niche.

IV. EC COOPERATIVE GOVERNMENT AND COMMERCIAL INITIATIVES

EUREKA (The European Research Coordination Agency)

Sometimes referred to as the French response to the American Strategic Defense Initiative (SDI), EUREKA (initiated in 1985) targeted the commercial applications of pure research done in the EC. In effect, EUREKA harmonizes R&D programs conducted throughout Europe (Austria, Switzerland, Sweden, Norway, Finland, Iceland, and Turkey are also included). The agency focuses on information technology, robotics, biotechnology, telecommunications, and energy. Over 300 projects have been conducted by more than 1,600 companies who, on average, bear 65 percent of the project cost. EUREKA is the umbrella for many other programs, JESSI (see below) among them.

Among EUREKA's most prominent initiatives is its HDTV project, EU-95. Its budget is $720 million, about 40 percent of which is financed by the EC member governments. In this effort to create and propagate a European high definition TV standard for the rest of the world, the EC has developed technology which is compatible with existing European television technology (PAL, SECAM). The new technology promises better picture quality at a cost dramatically lower than that of a new, Japanese HDTV set. HDTV is scheduled to have a full-fledged unveiling at the 1992 Olympics in Spain. Philips and Thomson have been the prime hardware participants in the project while national broadcasters cooperate on the development of systems.

In mid-1990, ninety-one new projects were added to the 294 existing EUREKA projects. The total budget is now $9.5 billion. Former Eastern Block countries will also be allowed to participate in the initiative. Among the European subsidiaries of American-based companies participating in EUREKA programs are General Motors, AT&T, Digital Equipment, and IBM (Figure 34). Only IBM has been accepted as a participant in a more competitively sensitive project (JESSI).

AIG (Airbus Industries Group)

A cooperative aircraft manufacturing venture of Germany's MBB (now owned by Daimler-Benz) with 37.9 percent ownership, France's Aerospatiale with 37.9 percent, British Aerospace with 20 percent and CASA of Spain with 4.2 percent, AIG was created in 1969 to combat the market dominance of America's Boeing Company. Subsidized to the tune of as much as $10 billion dollars over its lifetime, it now seems to be reaching an operating break-even level. The combination of AIG's new orders and its 800 aircraft backlog has led to the hope that by 1994 Airbus will deliver 40

**FIGURE 34:   EUREKA PROGRAM PROJECTS
(THROUGH JUNE, 1989 PHASE)**

Research Category	% of Total Funding
Robotics & Automation	21.2 %
Medical Applications & Biotechnology	18.2 %
Information Technology	15.8 %
Environmental Technology	10.4 %
Advanced Materials	10.1 %
Microelectronics	5.7 %
Lasers	5.1 %
Transportation	4.7 %
Energy	4.4 %
Communications	4.4 %
Total	100.0 %

Source: "The Eureka Initiative in Europe. Implications for Technology
Policy in the United States, " Kirkor Bosdogan, March 5, 1990

percent of the world share of all wide-body airliners.
AIG's target is 30 percent of the world jet airliner
market, vs. Boeing's 60 percent.

By using the Boeing "family" product marketing
concept, AIG has been able to find a market niche for
the replacement of aging Lockheed L1011's and DC
10's, of which there are nearly 700 now in service.
Boeing had never produced a product to fill that niche.
AIG has also succeeded with a gamble on newer computerized technology. While it is a little late for Boeing,

the EC will, in the context of the Uruguay Round of GATT, end production subsidies for Airbus.

ESA (European Space Agency)

ESA is the operating arm of a consortium of European countries in business to design and coordinate the construction of satellite and launching systems. The thirteen members of the consortium are Austria, Belgium, Denmark, France, Germany, Ireland, Italy, the Netherlands, Norway, Spain, Sweden, Switzerland, and the United Kingdom.

IMP (Integrated Mediterranean Program)

The EC has provided funding, in the form of this structural program, for the benefit of its less developed southern region (Portugal and Spain).

MAT-2

Italy's notoriously poor telecommunication system is being addressed by this EC funded infrastructure project, the objective of which is to link the Eastern Mediterranean countries with Italy.

NMTS (Nordic Mobile Telephone System)

While not an effort of the EC, NMTS, begun in 1982, provides statistical research support for the pan-European mobile telephone system that the EC hopes to put in place. NMTS has a single operator and no reselling of air time. Its value to the EC has been in its ability to predict the growth in cellular demand all over Europe. Cellular penetration in Scandinavia is unusually high because its difficult climate makes fixed-line service especially troublesome.

In Norway and Sweden about 40 of every 1,000 people have cellular service. This is quite a bit higher than the rate in the UK, for example (14 out of every 1,000), or in Germany, France, Italy, and Spain where the combined average usage is only 3 for every 1,000 people.

JESSI (Joint European Submicron Silicon Program)

A research and development consortium, funded in part by the EC and in part by the participating companies, JESSI hopes to reverse the European semiconductor experience of low volume production and high cost. No foreign companies have been invited to participate in this research group, with the exception of IBM-Europe which, after all, has over 100,000 local employees. The development goals of JESSI are to overtake the U.S. and Japan in the semiconductor development race by 1996. Its major participants are ST (SGS-Thomson), Siemens, and N.V. Philips. The member governments and the EC fund 50 percent of JESSI research on a project-by-project basis, while the companies provide the rest. Research is conducted separately by each company and then shared through a licensing process.

Smaller companies are using JESSI money to build their own R&D. For example, Matra MHS, the French, state-owned electronics and defense company, puts 25 percent of its revenue into R&D, 40 percent into process development and advanced engineering and the rest into new products and applications. JESSI will help focus and build their R&D. Cambridge Instruments needs JESSI funding to keep the electron-beam equipment company from falling out of the technology race and going belly-up. American companies are banging on the door because they want the information flow and industry contacts that membership can bring—but they proclaim no fear that the pace of technological development will threaten their own.

BRITE (Basic Research on Industrial Technologies for Europe)

This basic industrial R&D program now involves more than 400 private European companies, research institutes and universities. Each is involved in funded research in manufacturing technologies such as computer-aided manufacturing, lasers, or power generation.

ESPRIT (European Strategic Program for Research & Development in Information Technology)

Established in 1984 to do "pre-competitive" research in the information technology field, ESPRIT is a funded program which underwrites (on a matching fund basis) approved research proposals. Its first phase, worth nearly 1.5 billion ECU, was completed in 1988 with some marginally interesting results. The program now has a 3 billion ECU budget through 1993. Over 200 industrial participants worked on the development of information processing chips, a common software development system (Bull, GEC, IC, Nixdorf, Olivetti, Siemens), and an expert systems language for use in automotive applications.

RACE (R&D in Advanced Communications Technology for Europe)

Backed by $50 million of EC annual funding, RACE is another pre-competitive R&D program, specifically aimed at creating common standards within Europe for integrated, "broadband" voice, videotext, and graphics communications. By developing the groundwork for the introduction of integrated, high-speed telecommunications networks and broadband communications, RACE sets the stage for applications oriented work.

ECIS (European Committee for Interoperable Systems)

Focused primarily on the needs of smaller and medium-sized European companies, ECIS is basically a lobbying organization in technical fields. Its primary interest has been in protecting the ability of its members to do "reverse engineering" in the creation of new and competing software products.

Without this ability (by copyright law) such companies fear that they would no longer be able to participate in the growth of the systems integration market. As such they would be completely at the mercy of a few big American software vendors. The significance of this issue extends beyond European borders. It is generally acknowledged that Europe will set the pattern for what happens elsewhere in the world.

Two camps line up on opposite sides of the issue: The IBMs, Digital Equipments, Microsofts, and Lotus's of the world fear that a weak copyright law in Europe will reduce their dominance globally. They want interface specifications included in the copyright protection (it has not been to date). The lesser lights in this market (Groupe Bull of France, Olivetti of Italy, Fujitsu of Japan, NCR, and Unysis of the U.S.) fear that they will be locked out of the reverse engineering from which they derive many rival products. The specifications in question are needed by the marketplace in order to capitalize on the development of OSI (open system interchange).

This is no small business, with the world software market growing at more than 20 percent per year. The 1988 European packaged software market was over $16 billion and is expected to reach $30 billion by 1991 (International Data Corporation). Software revenue represents 35 percent of all computer industry revenue now and could represent as much as 50 percent of industry revenue by 1995.

V. EC POLICY INSTRUMENT TERMINOLOGY

EEIG (European Economic Interest Grouping)

This is one of two new legal business structures being promulgated by the EC in order to accommodate the need for corporate cooperation across borders as well as in new and far larger markets. The EEIG allows two or more independent companies or groups to pool their various resources and skills in carrying out common activities—while avoiding the usual antitrust ramifications of such cooperation. The cooperating companies must have no more than 500 employees and be EC based. U.S. subsidiaries, based in the EC, may participate and thereby benefit from economies of scale in purchasing, sales or R&D. Some in the EC see the EEIG as a way for smaller companies to join forces and develop products or strategies that will be effective, not only in the EC, but in North America as well.

ECS (European Company Statute)

This second corporate legal form allows for the creation of a single, pan-European, corporate structure, unfettered by the laws of individual member states—something akin to a national charter vs. a state charter in the U.S.. While registration is simplified, so are operational and legal concerns. Tax advantages could be gained from the consolidation of European financial reporting under the ECS.

UCITS (Undertakings for Collective Investments in Transferable Securities)

Comparable to an open-ended mutual fund in the U.S., a UCITS can be freely marketed anywhere in the EC. As an operational matter, such fund shares are typically marketed to institutions in Europe rather than to individuals.

ECU (European Currency Unit)

The ECU is the product of a basket of European currencies, used originally for budgeting purposes, but now as a financial instrument by companies, individuals, and institutions. The ECU represents the single European currency that many long for but may not see soon—and when it arrives, it's likely to have a considerably more fashionable name.

EMS (European Monetary System)

EMS is a system of bi-lateral currency exchange rates (parity rates) between European trading partner currencies. In principle, exchange rate fluctuations are minimized by controlling the deviations in bi-lateral currency rates and the central exchange rate. Participating members are generally permitted a 2.25 percent fluctuation, after which point, central banks must intervene if they are to protect the integrity of the central rate (ECU). After much ado, the U.K. agreed to join in late 1990.

EFTA members Norway, Sweden, Switzerland, and Austria have inquired about associate membership. Each is taken by the stability of a monetary system that has required only one minor realignment (in the late 1980s).

EMU (European Monetary Union or Economic and Monetary Union)

In striving for a single, united European economy, M. Delors and others within the Community are approaching EMU in three stages. The first stage, free capital movement, has been largely accomplished. The second, a European central banking system, is coming progressively closer, particularly with the concessions made by the U.K. in mid-1990. The third, fixed exchange rates and a common European currency, once thought impossible by most practical Europeans, is now within sight.

Excluded Sectors

The EC legislative process has specifically excluded four industry sectors from general competitive guidelines and directives. Separate directives and regulations have been propagated for the energy, water, transportation, and telecommunications industries. Each is so closely tied to the concerns of its host country, that for the most part, these four industries have been under complete government control—with regard to public procurement, for example. Decontrol of these massive public activities under conditions corresponding to those of smaller, already privatized industries might cause severe public dislocations.

Minitel, a profitable, state-run French videotext system, has caused a policy disagreement within the EC over opening competition in basic data services to private operators. France is holding out for restrictive licensing arrangements, while the U.K. and Germany want unencumbered competition. The 50 percent local content rule that has been included in procurement directives has been fought viciously by the EC's trading partners in the GATT forum, but it accurately reflects the fear by European bureaucrats of loss of central control over the excluded sectors.

CAP (Common Agricultural Policy)

In an effort to prop up the grossly inefficient European farmer, the EC has created agricultural production targets and marketing mechanisms designed to manage trade within the EC and with the rest of the world.

MCA (Monetary Compensation Amounts)

MCA's are agricultural subsidies (comparable to price supports in the U.S.) which are paid to food producers in order to reduce the relative effects of currency exchange where such distortions would otherwise influence the movement of agricultural products. As export subsidies, these payments are an impediment to free trade and have been a subject for discussion during the Uruguay Round of GATT. Then U.S. Agriculture Secretary, Clayton Yeutter called the EC "intransigent" over this topic which threatened GATT's 1990 deadline.

SME (Small & Medium Enterprise Task Force)

Established in 1986 by the European Commission, this group provides special assistance to small businesses and monitors EC proposals that may have an effect on them.

B-CNET (EC Business Cooperation Center)

This is an example of the effort being made on the part of the EC to include the little guy in the growing marketplace now available to the pan-European businessman. B-CNET helps put smaller companies in touch with each other in an effort to match up compatible business partners.

GSM (Groupe Special Mobile)

A mobile telephone consortium of European PTT's, GSM is pushing for system standards which can accommodate data, visual, and voice transmission. There are currently six different mobile telephone systems in operation in Europe, and all are largely incompatible. There were eighteen European cellular networks in operation in 1989.

GSM was created from CEPT (see above) in order to keep the mother group competitive in cellular technology. Ultimately, the new digital, pan-European cellular system will eclipse the existing analog systems, which cannot handle the rapid growth in capacity demand.

POTS (Plain Old Telephone Service)

Europe's phone systems are so old that they are fondly viewed by competitors from North America and the far East as antiques.

ERDF (European Regional Development Fund)

This regional economic development plan provides funds to depressed areas in order to subsidize their infrastructural development. "Objective 1" regions include Ireland, Greece, Portugal, much of Spain, and southern Italy, and get 80 percent of the funding. "Objective 2" regions are declining industrial areas such as the Ruhr Valley of Germany, Northern France, and certain industrial areas in England and Scotland. The Japanese have already begun to take advantage of the program.

SAP (Social Action Program)

SAP contains forty-seven proposals which support the principles of workers' rights as laid out in the Social Charter of the EC. Among the areas covered by these proposals are company reporting procedures, employee rights, and employee participation in company management.

VI. OTHER TERMINOLOGY

ONP (Open Network Provision)

In order to harmonize the technical interconnection standards of member states, telecommunications organizations are subject to regulations that provide a framework for the confluence of the conditions of use, tariffs, and technical interfaces to national telecom networks. The telecommunications organizations must, by law, give private operators standard access to public networks.

Service Directive

The service directive calls for free competition in value added services such as electronic data interchange, electronic mail, and other data communication services by 1993. The major U.S. players in value-added services (GE, IBM, Telenet, Infonet Services) have a lot at stake. They fear that the PTT's can still restrict entry into their markets by requiring costly compliance for interconnections or for leased lines.

Eurosclerosis

This popular euphemism was coined by West German economist Herbert Giersch and describes the state of the European economy from the late 1970s through the mid-1980s. The economic stagnation of that period has now been replaced by Single Market "Europhoria." The GDP growth of the European Community is now running at a 3—3.5 percent pace which is double that of the earlier period. For ten years Europe had been stuck at a growth rate of about 2 percent.

VCR (Video Cassette Recorder)

Along with a constitution, the VCR is single most desired possession of the citizens of Eastern (read: Central) Europe. The VCR is either the primary cause or primary effect of the rejection of Soviet-style communism.

SAD (Single Administration Document)

This single, multi-page customs document has, since 1988, replaced over 100 separate customs transit forms that were required when shipping products into and across EC borders.

Cross-Country Marketing

Companies from the U.S. and within the EC are adopting the old U.S. "major account" marketing approach as they expand or rationalize business across the EC. This allows a single sales and service team to call on and address all branches of a single company within Europe, regardless of the branch location. In the U.S. this strategy has carried with it the drawback of distance. In the EC, legal, travel, cultural, and language barriers have been standing in the way. With barrier-free borders, industry consolidation, and company rationalization, this strategy takes on new weight.

Global Company

Truly global companies view the world as their marketplace. Operations are not limited by geography, language, or culture. Overall strategy is global while substrategies aim at individual market segments. Within a corporate strategy and culture, subsidiaries, operating in their "home" markets, have a great deal of independence. The successful operating strategy is built on intra-company communication.

Pan-European Company

Until recently, most pan-European companies were American or Japanese. The fractured cultural markets of Western Europe effectively prevented European companies from growing beyond their borders. Even an industrial giant like Siemens, operating in over 300 different markets, generates nearly 50 percent of its revenue in its local market (Germany).

ISAC (Industry Sector Advisory Committee)

Groups of business representatives from one of several industries, ISACs are given the task of advising the U.S. Department of Commerce on trade policy issues. Simultaneously, they lobby the EC in Brussels in order to protect their business interests. The ISAC on services, for example, contains representatives from the air transport industry, information services, maritime, banking and securities, insurance, cinema and music industries.

Euro-Products

On the positive side, the offering of a single product across many regional markets promises economies of scale and cost savings in all phases of production and marketing (See IBM and Gillette for example). Nevertheless, the downside is the trap into which a company can fall by minimizing consumer choice and ignoring cultural affinities through product uniformity (Is your washing machine top-loading? Can it be adapted?).

Garlic Belt

This "sun belt" of Europe includes Spain, Italy, and Greece.

Fourth Criterion

When introducing a new product in the EC, companies are going to have to begin thinking in terms of the socio-economic impact of that new product. This Fourth Criterion follows the three primary considerations of safety, efficiency, and quality.

The concept has been prominently applied to the biotechnology product area. Bovine Somatotropin (BST) is a substance used to boost the production of dairy cows in the U.S. The EC, without any documentation, has precluded the import of the substance or affected animals and their products into Europe, largely in response to the demands of the Green party and its newly informed public. Meeting the Fourth Criterion test could restrict any number of products with which questionable compounds have come in contact.

CE Mark (Communaute Europeenne)

This Europe-wide product certification mark would be comparable to a UL listing in the U.S. and accepted in all member states without the requirement of further certification.

Genuine Community Link

A largely discredited, protectionist device, the Genuine Community Link would require majority community ownership of enterprises benefiting from EC directives in the excluded sector of transportation. Requiring a trucking company to take on a equal or majority partner from within the Community before allowing him the ability to access certain shipping markets would have locked out many non-EC freight haulers, for example. With the exclusion of the Genuine Community Link clause from the trucking cabotage directive, this worry was temporarily eliminated.

The slow-moving deregulation of the air cargo business still includes a Genuine Community Link clause in its proposed directive.

Social Dumping

In the short-term, many feel that EC companies will relocate to countries in which wages are lower and labor is less well organized. The American experience has shown that the effect of a single market is labor-leveling to some extent.

Strategic Alliances

A cooperative arrangement between companies to further the strategic goals of each, a strategic alliance can take the form of a joint venture, research agreement, cross licensing, or other long-term contractual understanding.

Endnotes

Chapter 1

1. Steve Lodge, "Language not the Only Jobs Barrier," *The European*, July 2, 1990.

Chapter 4

1. The European Community Information Service.

2. Japanese Ministry of Finance.

3. "Italy Hooks TI, but Angers Native Son," *Electronic Business*, April 30, 1990.

4. USTR Europe, 1992xn, p.9.

5. U.S. Department of Commerce, Trade Statistics.

6. Susan E. Kuhn, "Eager to Take on the World's Best," *Fortune Magazine*, April 23, 1990, p.71.

7. Jeffrey Bairstow, "Why Aren't You in Europe?" *Electronic Business*, December 11, 1989, p.132.

8. Kate Bertrand, "Scrambling for 1992," *Business Marketing*, February 1989, p.49.

9. *Euro-Report*, Prognos AG, 1989, Volume A, p.19.

10. "Big Spanish Firms Seek Latin Ties," *International Herald Tribune*, July 6, 1990.

Chapter 6

1. Jonathan Fuerbringer, "1992 Continues to Spur European Merger Pace," *International Herald Tribune*, July 6, 1990, p.13, taken from Translink's European Deal Review.

2. Europe, S.A., Agence Internationale D'information pour la Presse, September 22, 1990.

3. David Pitt-Watson, "Why a Joint Venture?" *Joint Ventures*, London: (Eurostudy Publishing Company, 1990).

4. *Ibid*, quoting a study by Professor Deigin Morris of INSEAD covering all mergers announced in the financial press from 1979—1985.

5. Monci Jo Williams, "Rewriting the Export Rules," *Fortune Magazine*, April 23, 1990, p.89.

6. J.P. Killing, "How to Make a Global Joint Venture Work," *Harvard Business Review*, May—June 1982, p.120.

7. I.J. Reynolds, "The Pinched Shoe Effect of International Joint Ventures," *Columbia Journal of World Business*, Summer 1984, p.23.

8. Ellyn Spragins, "Globetrotting for Dollars," *Inc. Magazine*, August 1990, p.116.

Chapter 7

1. Kate Bertrand, "Scrambling for 1992," *Business Marketing*, February 1989, p.54.

2. Kenneth Labich, "American Takes on the World," *Fortune Magazine*, September 24, 1990, p.40.

3. "European Telecom Markets are Open for Business," *Electronic Business*, January 22, 1990, p.57.

4. Electronic Business, April 16, 1990, p.70.

5. Barbara Berkman, "Semiconductors," Electronic Business, January 22, 1990, p.43.

6. European Community Information Service.

7. National Association of Computer Dealers.

8. *Insurance 1992,* London: Eurostudy Publishing Company, 1990.

9. *Ibid*, "Marketing the Service," p.14.

10. Barry James, "Europe's Blighted Beaches," *International Herald Tribune*, July 6, 1990.

11. Paul Hemp, "Green Legislation Brings Promise of Financial Bonanza," *The European*, July 2, 1990.

12. Michael Quint, "U.S. Banks Retreat from Overseas," *International Herald Tribune*, July 6, 1990.

13. *Ibid.*

14. *European Mobile Communications*, Quarterly Report, 1988, issue 5.

15. Barbara Berkman, "U.S. Companies Mobilize to Answer Europe's Call," *Electronic Business*, March 19, 1990, p.147.

16. "Europeans Want More and More ATE—at a Lower Cost," *Electronic Business*, February 19, 1990, p.61.

17. Prognos AG, Basel, Switzerland.

18. Barbara Berkman, "Spate of Mergers Challenges Europe's Top Companies," *Electronic Business*, January 22, 1990, p.53.

19. *EC 1992: Growth Markets*, U.S. Department of Commerce, International Trade Administration, September 1989, p.59.

20. Advertising Research Foundation, New York.

21. *Sports Illustrated*, June 1990.
22. European Community Information Service.
23. John Goff, "How a Bad Acquisition Blew Ferranti Out of the Defense Business," *Corporate Finance*, June 1990, p.46.

Chapter 9

1. *Electronic Business*, October 15, 1988, p.41.
2. Department of Commerce, International Trade Statistics.
3. Leigh Bruce, "High-Level Forum has Cautious Global Outlook," *International Herald Tribune*, July 2, 1990.

Chapter 10

1. *Electronic Business*, April 30, 1990, p.64.
2. "Monsanto's Design for Europe 1992," *Corporate Finance*, June 1990, p. 52.
3. *Electronic Business*, July 9, 1990, p.54.
4. "M&A's European Vacation," *Corporate Finance*, August 1990, p.39.
5. Martin Dickson, "Smith Corona Hits the Wrong Key," *Financial Times*, July 6, 1990, p.12.

Chapter 11

1. Gregory Millman, "A Belgian Charter Airline Prospers by Hedging Everything," *Corporate Finance*, July 1990, p.56.

Chapter 12

1. The examples of Syntech, ABC, DEF, Brainchild, and Intelligencia are actual case descriptions contributed by Dr. Ernst Lebsanft of Synlogic AG, Basel, Switzerland. The names of these four firms have been changed for the purposes of these examples.

2. Barbara Berkman, "Viewlogic Grows in Europe," *Electronic Business*, September 3, 1990, p.63.

3. Barbara Booth, "Balancing Overseas Sales Costs," *North American International Business,* August 1990, p.45.

4. *Ibid*, Virginia Citrano, "The One Million Dollar Lesson," p.31.

Chapter 13

1. R.C. Longworth, "Mideast Crisis Delivers Body Blow to E. Europe," *Chicago Tribune*, September 16, 1990.

2. "A New Kind of Soviet Threat," *Fortune Magazine*, November 5, 1990, p.13.

3. Dean Witter Reynolds, Inc., Prospectus, Dean Witter European Growth Fund.

4. *Kellogg World*, Summer 1990, J.L. Kellogg Graduate School of Management, p.2. Taken from testimony by Kevin McDonald, management consultant, Newton, MA, to the Subcommittee on European Affairs of the Senate Foreign Relations Committee concerning U.S. economic assistance to Poland.

Chapter 14

1. U.S. Department of Commerce.
2. R.C. Longworth, "Ready or Not, Reform Coming for Czechs," *Chicago Tribune*, October 22, 1990, Section 4, page 3.

Chapter 15

1. John Kiser, "Tapping East European Brain Power can Pay Off," *NewsAction*, Northwestern University, IBD, Spring 1990, p.6.

Chapter 16

1. Margaret A. Elliott, "Who's Doing Deals East of the Elbe," *Corporate Finance*, May 1990, p.38.
2. Ibid, p.39.
3. Shawn Tully, "GE in Hungary: Let There be Light," *Fortune Magazine*, October 22, 1990, p.137.
4. Frederick V. Guterl, "Can ICL Make Money Selling Computers to the Soviets?" *Electronic Business*, August 20, 1990, p.60.
5. Kate Bulkley, "Marriott, Schwinn, US West Lead the Pack into East Europe," *Expansion Management*, March — April 1990, p.18.
6. Margaret Kirk, "When the Walls Come Tumbling Down," *Your Company*, American Express, Fall 1990, p.43.

Index

A

ABC Corporation, 174-175

Airline deregulation, 78, 80

Anti-trust legislation: in Europe, 30

Automobile industry: and the European market, 37-39, 56-57; and Voluntary Restraint Agreements, 248-249

B

Banking industry, and U.S. banks, 105-107

C

Captive manufacturing, 28

Cellular communication industry, Europe: U.S. penetration of , 111-113

Central Europe. *See* Eastern Europe

Chemical processing industry, Europe: and U.S. growth in, 161, 162

Common Agricultural Policy (CAP), 145, 258

Common Market. *See* European Community

Computer Systems Policy Project (CSPP), 89

Consulting industry, Europe: and U.S. executives, 105-107

D

Defense industry, Europe: future of, 123
Domestic origin, 244-245; and substantial transformation, 247

E

Eastern Europe: economic decline of, 185; and entry to Western Europe market, 196, 204, 206; and health care industry, 209; industrial output, 184; investment environment, 193-194, 196-197, 210; and market research, 197-200; and multinational companies, 203-206; per capita income, 191; U.S. investment in, 192; work ethic, 187
Economy, Europe: and cutting costs, 28-29; growth of, 141-142, 261-262; problems, 10-13, 185
Electrical Connector industry, Europe: segmented growth of, 113; and U.S. manufacturers, 153
Endress & Hauser (E&H), 156-157
Environmental industry, Europe: and pollution control, 103-104; size of 103
Ericsson, 152
Euro Fighter Aircraft (EFA), 122-123
European Community (EC): and the aviation system, 78-80; and the banking industry, 109; and the broadcasting industry, 119-120; and the cellular communications industry, 110, and competition policy, 29, 35-36; and cooperation, 134; and the freight market, 76-77; history of, 227-228, 238-239; and international competitiveness, 36-37; and protectionism, 31, 34-35, 80-81, 86-87, 88, 92-93, 96, 117, 138, 144, 196, 244-245, 258; structure of, 229-230; and technical standards, 233-236; and the telecommunications industry, 81-85, 235
European Economic Space (EES), 228-229
European Environmental Agency (EEA), 231-232
European Free Trade Association (EFTA), 228

About the Publisher

PROBUS PUBLISHING COMPANY

Probus Publishing Company fills the informational needs of today's business professional by publishing authoritative, quality books on timely and relevant topics, including:

- Investing
- Futures/Options Trading
- Banking
- Finance
- Marketing and Sales
- Manufacturing and Project Management
- Personal Finance, Real Estate, Insurance and Estate Planning
- Entrepreneurship
- Management

Probus books are available at quantity discounts when purchased for business, educational or sales promotional use. For more information, please call the Director, Corporate/Institutional Sales at 1-800-PROBUS-1, or write:

Director, Corporate/Institutional Sales
Probus Publishing Company
1925 N. Clybourn Avenue
Chicago, Illinois 60614
FAX (312) 868-6250